The Small Business Guide to Online Marketing

A step-by-step guide to growing your business online

By Lola Bailey

bw

bw

brightword

A Brightword book
www.brightwordpublishing.com

HARRIMAN HOUSE LTD
3A Penns Road
Petersfield
Hampshire
GU32 2EW
GREAT BRITAIN

Tel: +44 (0)1730 233870
Email: enquiries@harriman-house.com
Website: www.harriman-house.com

First published in Great Britain in 2013 by Harriman House.

Copyright © Harriman House Ltd.

The right of Lola Bailey to be identified as author has been asserted in accordance with the Copyright, Design and Patents Acts 1988.

ISBN: 978-1-908003-67-6

British Library Cataloguing in Publication Data

A CIP catalogue record for this book can be obtained from the British Library.

Contents

About the Author

Lola Bailey MA (HRM) has over 20 years' blue-chip experience in coaching, sales and market development and is an Affiliate Member of the Institute of Digital Marketing.

Lola is also a freelance writer who has successfully published and edited a small business magazine, and has been featured in local newspapers, as well as Enterprise Nation's 'bible' for small businesses, *Working 5 to 9*. She is an enthusiastic champion of start-ups, supporting their endeavours both offline and online. Her online business hub, where small businesses and start-ups can learn internet marketing strategies, can be found at **www.ihubbusiness.co.uk**. The site and its social media counterparts have been built using most of the techniques found in this book.

Lola lives in London and is married with two children.

eBook edition

As a buyer of the print edition of *The Small Business Guide to Online Marketing* you can now download the eBook edition free of charge to read on an eBook reader, your smartphone or your computer. Go to:

http://brightwordpublishing.com/smallbusinessonlinemarketing

or point your smartphone at the QRC below.

You can then register and download your free eBook.

www.brightwordpublishing.com

brightword

Acknowledgments

This book would have been incomplete without the very generous contributions made by several internet marketers, bloggers and social media experts. My particular thanks go to:

Dr Dave Chaffey, Smart Insights (**www.smartinsights.com**)

Robert Clay, Marketing Wizdom (**www.marketingwizdom.com**)

David Robinson, Red Evolution (**www.redevolution.com**)

Kat Williams, Rock N' Roll Bride (**www.rocknrollbride.com**)

Milly Kenny-Ryder, Thoroughly Modern Milly (**www.thoroughlymodernmilly.com**)

A Call to Action

The time has come for businesses of every type and size to have an effective online presence.

According to recent data from Internet World Statistics (December 2011; www.internetworldstats.com) there are an estimated 52.7 million people in the UK who are online – representing a staggering population penetration of 84.1%. This places the UK in third position for internet usage within Europe, behind only Germany and Russia.

Despite this, many UK small business sites remain undynamic; in reality they appear as brochure sites with very little done to actively market them online. Worse still, according to Google's 'Getting British Business Online' campaign, there are an estimated 1.5 million businesses in the UK that do not yet have a website. The important point here is that their customers are searching online for products, services and information. According to Jupiter Research, 80% of internet users find new websites by searching; not through the commonly cited 'word of mouth' from a friend or colleague. They do not even see it on a television advert or a billboard. What most people do is go on to Google, type in what they are searching for and go to the sites suggested by the search results.

Ergo, if little is done to encourage the process of being found on Google then a business will find it difficult to succeed.

Simply having a website, however, is not a marker for online success. A June 2010 study – commissioned by Thomson Local, to establish how well those UK businesses with websites were prepared for the increasingly competitive world of online competition – found that a significant proportion of businesses had inadequately invested in establishing their online presence. (Source: www.analyticsseo.com/blog/state-uk-business-websites-2010).

During my time as the editor of a successful lifestyle magazine aimed at helping small and medium enterprises (SMEs) and start-ups promote their offerings locally, it became clear to me why so many of these businesses resisted the opportunity to market themselves online as well as offline; many of them still did not have a website. Why? Preconceptions, myths and unanswered questions about the internet abound and provide the reasons behind the reluctance to embrace its vast potential to maximise marketing outcomes.

Examples of frequently cited concerns are:

- The belief that online marketing offers little more than traditional marketing methods.

- Feelings of inadequacy – including not knowing how to identify what is a real opportunity from what will reap no rewards or even cost money.

- Lack of knowledge and understanding of how to plan a strategy, set objectives and allocate resources.

- Fear of making costly mistakes.

Do you recognise any of these concerns? The purpose of this book is to move you forward from these challenges to a place where you feel confident and willing to embrace the incredible opportunities that lie in wait for you. This book uses simple language, which cuts through the jargon, along with step-by-step examples, case studies and interviews with experts in their field. At the back of the book you will also find a range of useful resources, including helpful websites and a jargon buster.

I hope that by reading this book the hitherto seemingly complex world of the internet will be much more accessible to you, and ultimately generate improved outcomes and of greater success for your business, at a fraction of the cost you may have expected.

The journey may not be an easy one, but neither should it be difficult. What I am confident of is that either way, you will be in a much better position to take advantage of a very exciting marketplace.

Chapter 1
Introduction to Internet Marketing

In this chapter you will be given:

- A model for understanding the internet marketing process – the RACE model.
- The differentiating characteristics of online consumers
- The benefits of growing your business online.
- The three most important secrets of online marketing success.

What is internet marketing?

Well, marketing is the art of selling more of your products or your services. That's my KISS (keeping it short n' simple) definition of its core; fuller definitions depend on who you ask.

Internet marketing (which is sometimes called *digital marketing*) refers to the use of digital technologies and communications for marketing outcomes. Or (if you prefer a longer definition), it is the practice of harnessing digital technologies and media, including web, email, databases, mobile/wireless and digital TV, to support marketing activities which are aimed at achieving the profitable acquisition and retention of customers. The practice relies on developing a planned approach to reach customers and migrate them to online services through ecommunications and traditional communications. Customers are retained through the business improving their knowledge about those customers, interacting with them and then delivering targeted communications and offerings that match their needs to them.

Tip

The terms internet and World Wide Web (WWW) are frequently used synonymously. In fact, the World Wide Web is just one application running on the internet. Email is another, different application that runs on the internet.

Perhaps the clearest model I have come across to explain the internet marketing process is the RACE framework. RACE is reproduced here with the kind permission of one of the UK's foremost digital marketers, Dr. Dave Chaffey:

"We created RACE on **www.smartinsights.com** to give a simple framework to help small and large businesses alike take advantage of the opportunities available from digital marketing. There are so many tools and tactics available that it's difficult to know where to start. We hope RACE gives a structure to help you review and prioritise when there are so many options, but some options work better than others."

1 REACH
Build awareness on other sites and in offline media and drive to web presences

KPIs:
- ✓ Unique visitors & fans
- ✓ Audience share
- ✓ Revenue or goal value per visit

4 ENGAGE
Build customer and fan relationships through time to achieve retention goals

KPIs:
- ✓ % active hurdle rates
- ✓ Fan engagement
- ✓ Repeat conversion

2 ACT
Encourage audience to interact with brand on its website or other online presence

KPIs:
- ✓ Bounce rate
- ✓ Pages per visit
- ✓ Product page conversion

3 CONVERT
Achieve conversion to marketing goals such as fans, leads or sales on web presences and offline

KPIs:
- ✓ Conversion rates
- ✓ Leads and sales
- ✓ Revenue and margin

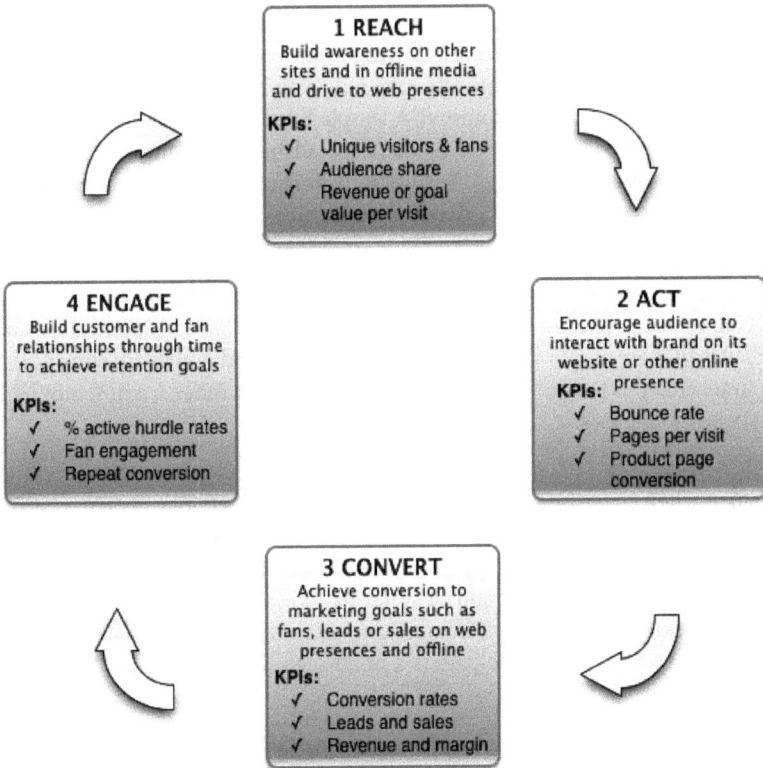

Source: www.smartinsights.com/digital-marketing-strategy/race-a-practical-framework-to-improve-your-digital-marketing

RACE consists of four steps, or online marketing activities, designed to help brands engage their customers throughout the customer lifecycle.

Key performance indicators (KPIs) are the measures that judge the performance of your business based on the success you wish to achieve. Examples of key performance indicators are: sales/revenues, cost of goods sold, number of products returned, number of new customers, number of sales calls made, number of downloads of your sales brochure, number of subscribers to your newsletter or the number of new website visitors. KPIs are therefore of great importance and I suggest you invest sufficient time to work out the KPIs you need to measure. In addition, it is important to determine what you will measure each of your KPIs against. For example, you could measure this month's sales against the previous month's results, or this month's sales against the same period last year. Doing this will help you understand the 'direction of travel' of your business – in other words, are you moving in the right or wrong direction? You will also need to work out how often the KPIs you have selected will need to be reviewed; daily, weekly or monthly? A simple Excel spreadsheet is all you need to record your KPIs. (Google has a online spreadsheet programme that multiple users can view and update. For more information on this feature visit **www.google.com/intl/en_US/drive/start/features.html**.

Step 1 – Reach: Reach means building an awareness of a brand, its products and its services on other websites and in offline media, in order to build traffic by driving visits to different web presences, such as your main site, microsites (small websites that are an off-shoot of the parent website, and which are considered a separate entity as they may present different content or indeed, a different URL) or social media sites.

Step 2 – Act: Act is about persuading site visitors to take the next step on their journey when they initially reach your site or social network presence. It may mean finding out more about your company or your products, searching to find a product or reading a blog post. It is about engaging the audience through relevant, compelling content and clear navigation pathways so that they don't hit the back button. The bounce rates on many sites is greater than 50%, so getting the audience to act or participate is a major challenge – which is why I have identified it separately.

Step 3 – Convert: Conversion is where the visitor commits to form a relationship, which will generate commercial value for the business.

Step 4 – Engage: Build customer relationships over time, to achieve retention goals.

Digital marketing should not be driven by technology; it should be driven by the business returns from gaining new customers and maintaining relationships with those customers.

Effective digital marketing rarely occurs in isolation; rather it is most effective when integrated with other communications channels, such as phone, direct mail or face-to-face. Online channels should be used to support the whole buying process, from pre-sale to sale, to post-sale and further development of customer relationships.

Characteristics of online consumers

In addition to having an understanding of what online marketing is all about, it is also important to understand the differentiating characteristics of online consumers:

- They comprise roughly an equal number of men and women.
- They tend to be sceptical of online marketing efforts.
- They are well-informed and discerning shoppers.
- They generally respond to targeted messaging.
- They generally reject messages aimed only at selling.
- They place great value on information.
- They like to control the information which they receive about products and the conditions under which they receive that information.
- They are the ones who will give permission to be contacted by you, and they are the ones who will control the resulting interactions with you.

Why should you seek to grow your own business online?

For you as a business owner, marketing your business online will help you to:

- **Grow your sales**: gain wider distribution to customers you cannot reach offline, display a wider product range than in-store, and/or offer better prices.
- **Add value**: give your customers greater benefits and guide new product developments through online dialogue and feedback.
- **Get closer to your customers**: reach your customers with online tools that can help you discover what your potential customers are searching for. Create a two-way dialogue; ask them questions, conduct online interviews, monitor chatrooms, forums and social media sites to learn more about your customers.
- **Save money**: provide a virtual customer service, use online transaction administration and track your success at little or no cost.
- **Extend your brand online**: provide a new position and a new experience for your customers online, whilst retaining your brand's familiarity.

Increasingly, customers like to hang out and spend their money – and time – on the web. It is a marketplace in its own right. When shopping or buying a product, most consumers will look to the web as a primary influencer and decision tool. Even in the non-digital world, it is quite common to go into a store and find prospective customers surfing the web on their smartphones in search of lower prices at competing stores. In spite of the many advantages of online marketing, it remains true that the failure rate of businesses here is high. So how can you be better placed to succeed? The best wisdom I can give you is that you should not so much expect success, but prepare for it. At the back of this book you will find helpful tools, resources and frameworks to help you succeed in your internet marketing journey. Are you ready? I hope so!

Successful online marketing

The three most important secrets of online success are:

1. Content analysis
2. Search analysis
3. Performance measurement.

1. Content analysis

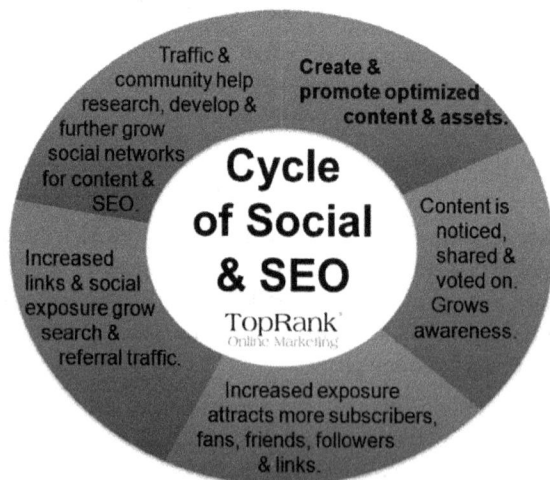

Source: www.flickr.com/photos/toprankblog

The above image shows the cycle of content creation, search engine optimisation (SEO) and promotion via social networks that facillitate a continued insight into content marketing. Read more at: **www.toprankblog.com/2010/05/beyond-google**.

Spend any amount of time on social media and you will invariably come across the oft-repeated maxim 'Content is King'. It's true. But what is this mysterious 'Content'?

For internet marketers, content is any kind of material you create on behalf of your business. This could include a simple advert, a YouTube video, a Facebook page, a SlideShare presentation, a Tweet or Twitter promotion, a mobile app – anything, in essence, that aims to attract people who are potential customers. If it leads them towards your brand and to greater levels of engagement with your brand or business, then it must be good.

Online, it is less about pushing out messages and more about pulling in customers and potential customers. This is done through material that entertains, amuses, informs and serves a function, but also answers a need. In some way the material must provide added value to such an extent that it is welcomed, asked for again and shared with others. The traditional model of advertising – of promotional messages – has been used since the genesis of time by marketers and is based on this premise: in exchange for subsidising content produced by a third party broadcaster, publisher etc., the advertiser earns the right to interrupt the consumer's experience with adverts. This is the case with television advertising. Online, however, customers simply click it away. They are becoming increasingly resistant and hard-to-win-over to advertising messages of this sort, resulting in a gradual erosion of trust in the advertisers themselves.

Time was, when everything and everyone had a defined role. There were those who produced, those who consumed and those who paid. Online however, everyone is a content producer, consumer and payer. We see 'consumers' creating their own content in the form of blogs, videos, and photos posted to Flickr. They create branded videos on YouTube, they write customer ratings and reviews, publically declaring themselves as "fans" and openly discussing good and bad product experiences. Consumers now 'own' brands, virtually. Companies that originally dismissed social media as a serious marketing tool now ensure they have a distinct presence on all social media sites. Marketers are bypassing the middlemen and are creating content themselves, to get ever closer to, and in more direct contact with, the selected audience, as well as gather vital data for future marketing initiatives. Entertaining YouTube videos, information-orientated how-to microsites, useful mobile apps and a variety of other services that only conceptually relate to their brand – and are not meant to directly sell the product (yet) – are all developed by present-day internet marketers.

Online, it is the best material which will pull in the right people; those who are most likely to buy your product or service and tell others about it, eventually becoming your advocates. In a crowded market place your content must be outstanding in order to stand out.

2. Search analysis

So, you have managed to create lots of outstanding content. Is that enough? No! The next step in the process is to have a search strategy in place. This allows potential customers to find your content online. Most clicks are made on the first page of Google, so therefore, this is where you need to be.

Sadly, there are still too many people who believe all they need to do is build a website and let their designer get the site well placed with search engines. "Can't I just pay someone to register the site with lots of search engines?" is a question I have been asked on many an occasion. The short answer to this is no. The proliferation of advertising offering to guarantee top ten placements in a gazillion search engines – no doubt aimed at the very people likely to ask this question – has given rise to this misconception.

Search engine optimisation (SEO) – the practice of getting your content found online – isn't rocket science, but unfortunately neither is it child's play.

The overwhelming majority of sites do not have a chance in the search engine rankings, simply because they make simple mistakes. Designers need to make the websites they build easy for search engines like Google to find and index. The role of metadata, links, keywords – all the things you are going to learn about in this book – are necessary for good SEO results.

3. Performance measurement

"You cannot generate sustainable improvements without measurement."

– Lola Bailey

In our knowledge-based society, information is power. Tracking your key performance indicators – as I have briefly discussed already – is particularly important, as doing this will enable you to concentrate on the elements of your business that lead to increased sales. Happily, there are several programmes online that will help you measure just how well your business is doing. In spite of this, many of the small businesses I have worked with do not track their performance. The top reasons cited by them for not tracking their performance indicators include "too many metrics", "confusion", and "not knowing how to do it". Most people know they want a return on investment but are not sure how to measure this return. In this book, I will show you how and why you should track your performance using the free programme, Google Analytics.

Chapter 2

The Importance of Superior Content

We have touched on the importance of content for your business, so now lets look at how you can structure your content, so that it offers your blog or your website the best chances of getting found. In this chapter you will be given:

- A simple framework for writing your website content.
- Ways to generate content for any business.
- An introduction to blogging and its benefits.
- Expert interviews – blogging.

A simple framework for writing your website content

Give your content a unique voice

Think of ways to offer solutions to a need that is not being addressed, or a better way to meet a need. Listen to the everyday conversations that are being had about your product or niche and visit relevant forums to identify common themes and potential opportunities. One of the key reasons why businesses online do not reap their potential is due to the lack of good quality content on their sites. So how can you avoid this?

Make sure your content is useful

Think about how you can create content that answers a practical question from the customer that they may not ordinarily think of asking you. The idea here is to answer the question: "What else can you do for me?" To help you brainstorm ideas, here are a few suggestions of what your content could offer:

Convenience: What can you offer to your customer that will be giving them the benefit of convenience? For example, could you suggest a number of alternative routes to your nearest retail outlets to them? Could you give your customer an alternative means of viewing a key event which they are unable to attend, such as a link to a blog or a video of the event?

Easily shared: How can you ensure your content is shared? Could you have an inviting competition on your website that encourages those entering the competition to seek votes from their friends, thereby drawing others to your content?

Effective: What can you offer to your customer that will be effective in bringing them back to your site? For example, if you are a retailer of outdoor sports clothing, could you also offer regional/local forecasts? Skiers are very likely to purchase outdoor sportswear; giving them access to local or regional weather conditions will be an effective pull strategy.

Time-enhancing: What can you offer that will save time for your customers? For instance, could you offer a range of delivery options?

Throughout it all, you must be subtly promoting your brand. For example, if you are targeting the weight loss market, you could post lots of low-fat recipes or create a computer application that helps dieters analyse their current eating habits and then offer practical ways to reduce their fat intake or offer easy ways to increase fruit/vegetable intake. (This has probably already been created!)

Write content that will be memorable

Memorable content has lasting value and will gain you more fans. There are several ways to do this:

- Make the content entertaining, through being fun and easier to read.

- Appeal to the emotional aspect of a need with a strong call to action – emotional hooks are extremely powerful – try to invoke a similar, strong reaction with your content.

- Include metaphors and analogies, which are great for bridging the gap between heart and head. Analogies are *the* best recipe for creating a great blog post; by being sure all of your ingredients are present in the correct amounts and added at the right time. (Hopefully you have seen what I just did there!)

- Shine a spotlight on your achievements – e.g. awards you have won, testimonials, 'big names' that have used your brand – most of us have an ego and want to be associated with the best.

- Demonstrate how your product or service can help improve the lives of your customers, for example, through testimonials, an "Is this you?" quiz, etc.

How to generate content for any business

It's one thing to know you need to create content for your blog or website, but where do you start? Take your pick!

If you haven't already, have a look at **Google Alerts** (**www.google.com/alerts**). Set an alert with a few industry keywords, and ask it to deliver at least twenty stories a day. Read the headlines and copy interesting links into a file for future use. When you get several related stories, you've got an instant roundup piece.

Skim national and local **newspapers** and **magazine stories**. How does the news impact on your readers? Write about national trends, and you will soon be thought of as an authority. You could also visit Yahoo! Buzz and Google Trends to learn what people are looking for – you might just get an idea for an article that could drive some search traffic your way.

Read **small publications** and **trade publications**. If your business is in a niche area, check the experts' columns in local papers or business weeklies. Few people outside your community will have read these, and their topics are often easily recycled.

Think **"a problem equals an opportunity"**. What are the biggest problems faced by your customers? Focus on topics that would provide balm to their wounds.

Tackle a **controversy**. Weigh in on your industry's hot topic. This can be especially effective if you have a different viewpoint to offer.

Ask a **question**. Is there an industry issue that you're undecided about? Discuss your mixed feelings.

Scan **social bookmarking sites**, such as Digg, StumbleUpon and Delicious. These are always great places to find buzz-worthy news to write about.

Review the developments in your niche. How has your industry changed in the past five years? Ten years? Look for milestones for reflection.

Create a **regular feature**. For instance, you could do a "Friday news roundup" every week or a "Tuesday tips".

Write a **book review**. Tell readers if the hot new book in your niche is insightful or inane.

Do a **product review**. As with the book review: good, bad or ugly?

Review websites related to your niche. The best and the ones which don't hit the mark, perhaps?

Visit **question and answer sites**. Listen for what is being asked about that you haven't answered yet. Try Yahoo! Answers or LinkedIn for starters.

Attend a local **community event**. Then write about it.

Set yourself a **topics challenge**. Tell yourself you need to come up with 50 topic ideas today. Jot down anything and everything.

Take the **one-hour challenge**. Similar to the idea above, challenge yourself to find a story idea within the next hour.

Run a **poll**. Register for an account with a site like **PollDaddy.com**, then publish a poll related to a topic you have written about.

If you have express written permission, you could **transcribe, or record an interview with a guest** that will be of interest to your readers. Do you have a favourite thinker in your space? Get in touch. You'll be surprised how many 'gurus' are up for a quick Q&A.

Using Google Keywords to generate content

The free **Google Keywords** tool can be very useful when it comes to generating new online content. Let's take a look at this marvellous tool in a little more detail. Google's keyword tool is a comprehensive online application that will give you ideas for your content by generating a list of words (called 'keywords') that are used by your potential customers when looking for particular information. By finding out what consumers are searching for, you find out what information holds value to them. To use the tool you will need to create a free account at **adwords.google.com.**

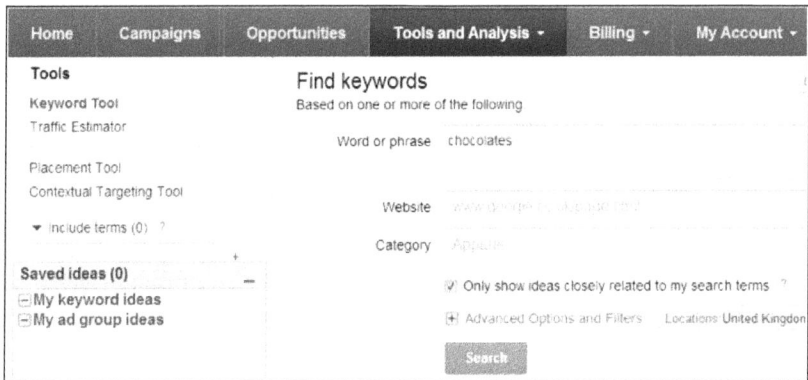

Then do the following:

In AdWords, click on '**Tools and Analysis**' to get a drop down menu and select '**Keyword Tool**'.

Imagine, for example, that you are a business wanting to write a blog post on chocolates.

Type two to four related keywords into the '**Find keywords**' section that you believe your customers might use to find information relevant to your subject. For now, let's use chocolates. You might choose to enter:

- gourmet chocolates
- organic chocolates
- diabetic chocolates
- chocolate making materials.

Search results are divided into two primary sections; 1. Search terms (the terms you have entered) and 2. Keyword ideas (Google's own suggestions based on your search – click on the '**More like these**' link to dig deeper).

Keyword Ideas	Ad group Ideas (Beta)			About this data
Download ▾			Sorted by Relevance ▾	Columns ▾
✓ Save all **Search Terms (4)**			1 - 4 of 4 ▾	
Keyword	Competition	Global Monthly Searches	Local Monthly Searches	
☐ gourmet chocolates ▾	Medium	22,200	1,900	
☐ organic chocolates ▾	High	1,900	210	
☐ diabetic chocolates ▾	High	6,600	2,900	
☐ chocolate making materials ▾	Medium	210	16	
✓ Save all **Organic (24)** - organic chocolate, organic chocolate gifts...			More like these	
✓ Save all **Gourmet Chocolate (54)** gourmet chocolate, chocolate gourmet...			More like these	
✓ Save all **Easter Egg (10)** chocolate easter eggs, diabetic easter eggs...			More like these	

On examining the list, some words may jump out at you – 'chocolate recipes', as shown in the screenshot below, tells me that there is a significant demand for chocolate recipes online with 368,000 local monthly searches. The competition for these keywords is ranked at 'low', which means that you stand a good chance of being found online if you use these terms within your content. Terms with low or medium competition are good; look out for these. If you are indeed selling chocolates, you may want to include chocolate recipes in your content and include those recipes that have large local monthly search volumes, i.e. are popular, such as chocolate truffle or hot chocolate recipes.

Keyword Ideas	Ad group Ideas (Beta)				
Add to account ▾	Download ▾	View as text ▾	View in Traffic Estimator ▾	Sorted by Relevance ▾	Columns ▾
✓ Save all **Search Terms (5)**				1 - 5 of 5 ▾	
Keyword		Competition	Global Monthly Searches	Local Monthly Searches	
☐ hot chocolate recipe ▾		Low	60,500	4,400	
☐ chocolate truffles recipe ▾		Low	33,100	12,100	
☐ chocolate truffle recipe ▾		Low	33,100	9,900	
☐ dark chocolate truffle recipe ▾		Low	880	140	
☐ chocolate recipes ▾		Low	2,240,000	368,000	

Narrow Your Search

Your earlier search will have given you a good starting point for some valuable keyword information, but the subject itself – chocolate – is very general in nature. A useful next step is to narrow your search down even further. For instance, you may want to improve the sales of your dark chocolate brands and to that end, your strategy might be to focus on the health benefits of dark chocolate. Once again, you will need to enter in a few keywords that you believe people might use to find information on dark chocolate, such as 'healthy dark chocolate', and then focus on the keyword suggestions from Google. Expanding (click on the + symbol next to the term) two of the keyword suggestions from the tool reveals the following:

Keyword ideas	Ad group ideas (Beta)				

					About this data
Add to account ▾	Download ▾	View as text ▾	View in Traffic Estimator ▾	Sorted by Relevance ▾	Columns ▾

✓ Save all	Search Terms (0)			

✓ Save all	Good For You (5)		More like these	1 - 5 of 5 ▾
Keyword		**Competition**	**Global Monthly Searches**	**Local Monthly Searches**
☐ is dark chocolate good for you ▾		Low	4,400	720
☐ is honey good for you ▾		Low	14,800	1,900
☐ dark chocolate good for you ▾		Low	4,400	720
☐ chocolate good for you ▾		Low	14,800	2,900
☐ is chocolate good for you ▾		Low	14,800	2,900

✓ Save all	Healthy (10)		More like these	1 - 10 of 10 ▾
Keyword		**Competition**	**Global Monthly Searches**	**Local Monthly Searches**
☐ healthy chocolate ▾		Low	49,500	3,600
☐ dark chocolate healthy ▾		Low	4,400	320
☐ chocolate healthy ▾		Low	49,500	3,600
☐ healthy sweets ▾		Low	8,100	880
☐ healthy dark chocolate brands ▾		Medium	320	18
☐ healthy dark chocolate ▾		Low	4,400	320
☐ healthy chocolate snacks ▾		Low	590	46
☐ healthy chocolates ▾		Medium	1,300	73
☐ dark healthy chocolate ▾		Low	4,400	320
☐ heart healthy chocolate ▾		Low	880	18

Previous to this search, you might have planned to write a piece for your blog or website entitled 'The health benefits of dark chocolate'. After seeing these keyword results, your knowledge of what your potential customers are actually interested in is more refined.

Implement What You've Learned

Your original blog headline was going to be: 'The health benefits of dark chocolate'. Although there is nothing inherently wrong with this headline, it does not take advantage of the information provided by the keywords tool about the search needs of potential visitors.

A more effective title, based on your research, would be: 'Seven reasons why chocolate is good for you'. It's all in the data (2900 local monthly searches, to be exact).

Beyond the Blog

Do not limit your good ideas to just a blog. Consider, for example, producing a short video of how dark chocolate is produced or different parts of the production process. Or, how about an interview with an 'expert' on the health benefits of chocolate? Providing you have the written permission of your interviewee, you could publish this on your website. The point is that once you get a creative idea that adds value to your content, find different ways to get it in front of your customer.

Blogging and its benefits

A blog can be a very powerful marketing communications tool – and an incredibly cheap one. There are several reasons to start a blog, which you will learn about in this section; perhaps the most common reason why businesses start blogs is because they enable dialogue with customers and help to 'personalise' customers' experience of a brand.

Creating a blog home page

I highly recommend content management systems for blogging. Simply put, a content management system (or CM system) is a system that allows you to independently manage the content of your website, without needing to know any complicated programming language. CM systems allow you not only to manage the content of your website, they will also provide you with the ability to approve and validate the content on your site before it goes live on the web. CM systems can also control the time a content element goes live, the day and time it is removed from the site and the locations on the site where the content element appears. Web pages are generated from templates. This allows your content writers to concentrate on what they do best – writing. Then, when they, or you, are ready to publish items to the website, the content will display the standardised branding of your site.

A good example of a content management system is WordPress. CM systems have outstanding capability (if using WordPress I suggest you go for the self-hosted version, which you can download at **wordpress.org**) – enabling you to service your marketing needs effectively and in a timely manner. Below is a snapshot of Ihubbusiness' homepage, a blog which was created in WordPress (**www.ihubbusiness.co.uk**).

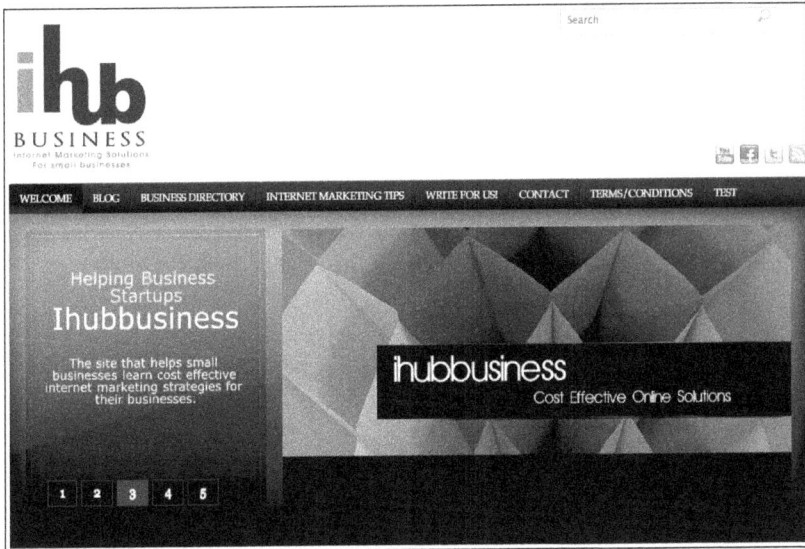

Your blog homepage is your welcome page for your blog. Here are two key considerations for your homepage:

What **image** do you want your blog to portray? Fun? Elegant? Serious? Think about how you want your brand to be thought of, and dig deeper to find out how you want your blog to look. Consider which fonts, images, etc. will work best with your chosen outcome.

Which **elements** do you feel are **important,** in order for your readers to feel comfortable about your blog? For example, blogs are generally expected to include the following information:

- Posts
- An 'About' section – this is sometimes at the footer of a blog
- A contact page
- Categories – these are the logical groupings of your posts. Categories are the means of sorting your blog posts into topics, to make it easier for visitors to search your blog.
- A blogroll – this is basically a list of links that appears in your sidebar. You can link to any site found on the internet in your blogroll; however, best practice is to link to those sites which are directly related to the content of your blog. Remember that you are in effect recommending

those sites to your readers as sources of related, reliable information, so choose carefully!

- Subscription options
- Logo.

Your logo can also serve as your 'avatar', or picture, when you post comments on other blogs or forums. You can also use it on marketing items, such as business cards.

As your blog grows in age you can add other elements, such as archives, recent posts and much more.

Creating a blog post

Your posts are the most important element of your blog. They should take up at least 75% of screen space on your blog's site. Blog posts appear in reverse chronological order, which means that your blog remains current and timely. The main elements of your blog posts should be:

1. Title

This is the most crucial part of your blog to get right. It is basically your headline; it needs to lure visitors in so they want to read more. Titles are also useful in terms of search engine optimisation; search engines value titles strongly in ranking results, and using popular and relevant keywords in your titles will help you drive more traffic to your blog.

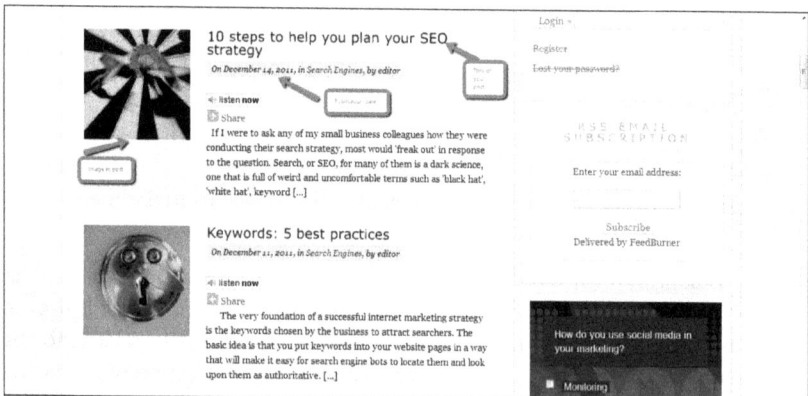

2. Publication date

It's all about being current on the internet, and visitors want to know that yours is an active blog that they can rely on for up-to-date information.

3. Introduction

This is possibly the second most important part of your blog. You can start your blog-introduction by, for example, asking a question or quoting an interesting statistic. Again, the idea is to have your visitors wanting to read on.

4. Body

Here is the meat of your article. It helps to include images to add colour and visual relief. Images can also act as another way you can drive traffic to your blog; many people perform keyword searches through search engines, for the purpose of finding images and pictures online. By labelling the images that you use in your blog post, being consistent with relevant keywords searches, you can drive some of that image-search traffic to your blog.

5. Links and Trackbacks

Your blog posts should contain links within your content. The purpose of these links are: firstly, to add value, or an extra dimension or depth to your information, by referring to sources of additional information; and secondly, to provide a way of letting bloggers (whose material you have referred to) know that you have done so in the form of a 'trackback'. A trackback generates a link on the other blogger's blog; it actually acts as an additional pathway for traffic to your blog, since readers on the referenced blog are likely to click on the trackback link and find your blog.

6. Blog comments

If your business is a full-time one, it is very important to enable comments on *your* blog. Comments are where your readers are given the opportunity to feedback and join in the conversation. By responding to comments left by your readers, you are demonstrating your commitment to them and this in turn will be rewarded by their loyalty to you. A word of caution however is that 'spammers' (people who send unwanted content, usually in large volumes) are rife on the internet. What this means is that you are likely to get comments that have no bearing whatsoever on your content. This is the reason why some bloggers turn comments off. However, if your business is a full-time one, comments are important. Plus, you can take a number of steps, through plug-ins for instance, to reduce the number of unwanted comments.

Plug-ins

A plug-in is a piece of software code that allows a programme to do something it is not able to do by itself. A good example of a plug-in is the commonly used Adobe Flash Player. Without Flash Player you wouldn't, for example, be able to view BBC News bulletins that are embedded into web pages.

There are many different types of plug-ins, accomplishing many different things. There are plug-ins for optimising your Google rankings, such as the 'All-in-one-SEO' plug-in, plug-ins for social media networking, plug-ins to prevent unwanted comments on your websites, and many more.

In fact, an abundance of plug-ins exist. Email programmes will use privacy plug-ins for security. Media players might need a plug-in to play a specific type of media. And so on. (Have a look in the Useful Resources at the back of the book for a comprehensive listing of plug-ins.)

Benefits your business can gain from blogging

Search engines love blogs. By posting high quality content and posting frequently, you will soon acquire a large amount of content that is rich in keywords. As a result, you will find your site becoming more prominent in online searches.

It encourages dialogue. Blogs are unlike standard websites, press releases or product brochures, in that they allow people to publicly respond. If you find some content on another blog particularly useful, for example, you will be able to leave a comment to that effect and usually with a link back to your own site. If your customers leave some feedback on your blog, you will have an opportunity to demonstrate your responsiveness to them, and establish a deeper connection.

Blogs allow you to continually showcase your expertise. Whatever it is that your small business does, you can blog about it passionately and often, demonstrating your authority in the field at the same time. This can allow your customers and potential customers to see you as something of an expert.

It can help you get media coverage. Journalists increasingly use blogs as a source of news stories. If you post sufficient high-quality content often enough, sooner or later you will come into the radar of a journalist looking for your opinion or comment on an issue.

It sharpens your thinking and helps you stay informed. The pressure to produce content often, and of a consistently high quality, will lead you towards thinking more deeply about your topics, and educating yourself further on those topics. To write well you have to read extensively – and allowing yourself to become out of date is not an option!

It gives you a dynamic platform to convey information about your company. Let's be honest – the traditional press release is, well, traditional. Do people still read press releases? We are now living in 'Generation Internet', a generation that wants to interact, share, be responded to, and be entertained.

It is a versatile medium. Your blog can be used to convey news, information, recall products, demonstrate a product, run a survey or poll, and much more.

Writing tips

According to Jakob Nielsen's seminal web usability study, people rarely read web pages word for word. The study found that 79% of users always scanned any new pages they came across. As a result, web pages have to employ scannable text using the following guidelines:

- Highlighted keywords
- Relevant sub-headings – not "clever" ones
- Bulleted lists
- One idea per paragraph
- The inverted pyramid style of writing; starting with the conclusion then supporting it with sentences that follow
- Half the word count – or less – than the 'control condition'.

The study also found that credibility in content can be increased by "high quality graphics, good writing and the use of outbound hypertext links". In addition, the study found that links to other sites "show that other authors have done their homework and are not afraid to let readers visit other sites". For more information on the study visit **www.useit.com/alertbox/9710a.html**.

Blogging expert interview: Thoroughly Modern Milly

Milly Kenny-Ryder

www.thoroughlymodernmilly.com

Milly Kenny-Ryder is a singer, fashionista, foodie, arts enthusiast, writer and blogger, living in London "excitedly making the most of this dynamic city". She began her blog, *Thoroughly Modern Milly*, in April 2010 and she also writes as a guest blogger for *Visit London*, *Coupobox* and as a special columnist for *On The Fringe*.

What made you decide to set up a blog?

I left university, moved home and realised pretty quickly how difficult it would be for me to get a job in the arts. So I accepted a well-paid administration job in a property company, promising myself that I would continue simultaneously a life in the arts; a blog seemed like a good way to keep that promise.

What are you trying to achieve with the blog? What sorts of things do you blog about?

It began as a creative outlet for me to share my enthusiasms, a diary for everything I am interested in and I hope will interest others. *Thoroughly Modern Milly* is a blog about music, theatre, art, food, fashion and lifestyle – mostly in London, but sometimes venturing further afield.

Who are your readers? What do think they get out of your blog?

Anyone and everyone. I have readers all over the world, some who I know of, others who are entirely anonymous. Some followers check in regularly, commenting and interacting, others stop by only once. I hope they are inspired and interested by my writing and, most of all, encouraged to go out and experience the things I write about.

What was the 'aha' moment that made you realise that this was more than just a hobby?

Strangely, it was at an event where I was given a press badge that said *Thoroughly Modern Milly* on it, rather than my full name. From that moment on I began to feel more like TMM than Milly, and I knew it was a vocation I wanted to pursue.

You are clearly passionate about blogging. Why do you think small businesses should be considering it? Is blogging right for everyone?

Blogging can be as private or public as the creator wishes; it is a very versatile medium and is growing fast. It is accessible to all, making it a brilliant business tool. I think blogging *can* be for everyone, if you have the right attitude. It is instant, so is able to instigate or announce trends; it is perfect for modern companies who wish to be of the moment.

Is it possible to make money from a blog? What are the criteria before this can be taken seriously?

Honestly, it is difficult to make money solely from blogging, but it is possible through effective advertising and promoting. There are few criteria; basically more traffic and page views means more money. You are probably more likely to make money by creating a profile from blogging and then going on to write a book.

How does blogging fit in with social media as a whole?

Funnily enough, I still feel very new to the social media world, despite blogging relentlessly for the last two years! I use Facebook and Twitter in conjunction with my blogging and find it immensely helpful to broaden my audience. Social media is evolving so quickly, there is always something new to learn. This is the area I would like to improve, as it can be a great tool for a blogger.

How should someone get started – practically speaking?

I would recommend Blogger or WordPress as blog sites to use. It is very quick and easy to set up the site, so think carefully about a good name, the visuals, design, font, etc. A good camera and reliable computer are a massive help.

What have been the changes you have seen since you started blogging?

I am braver now, more daring. Blogging has taught me to be a reviewer, journalist, critic, photographer, interviewer... and I am constantly learning on the job.

What are your top tips for people starting blogging?

Just go for it. I spent so long umm-ing and ahh-ing. Once I forgot about the daunting prospect of the world wide web audience, it was easy. Try to have a focus and set yourself simple goals; readers like continuity so posting regularly is important.

Blogging expert interview: Rock N' Roll Bride

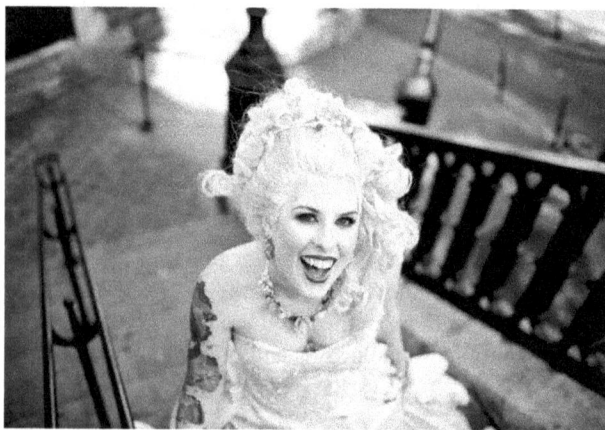

Source: Founder Kat Williams by David McNeil Photography

Rock N' Roll Bride is a UK wedding blog founded by Kat Williams and launched in October 2007. The blog began as a simple wedding planning site, but in 2009 was rebranded as a "Mecca for gorgeous photography and inspiring real weddings". *Rock N' Roll Bride* is an ever growing brand with magazine features, including *Marie Claire Magazine, Cosmopolitan Bride, The British Journal of Photography, Easy Living, Company, Tattoo Revolution, Perfect Wedding, Wedding Ideas, Wed Magazine, Southern Weddings Magazine (US)*, the *Guardian, The Sunday Times Style Magazine* (Ireland) and the *Daily Express*.

Rock N' Roll Bride was awarded Best Wedding Blog by *Cosmopolitan* in their Blog Awards which took place in October 2011.

What made you decide to set up a blog?

My story isn't that remarkable or different to that of many people who get into the wedding industry. I started my blog when I was planning my own wedding to Gareth in 2007. At the time I didn't even consider this could become a career; I simply wanted a place to collate all my wedding ideas and inspirations.

Throughout my planning I discovered American wedding blogs. I loved the instant nature of blogging – how you could comment and feel part of a community. I wanted to be a part of that. After my wedding was over I didn't want to give up weddings or blogging, so I decided to morph my blog into a place for alternative wedding inspiration. Although I loved the wedding blogs I'd found throughout my plans, none of them catered to the specific kind of bride or style of wedding that I wanted – the alternative, the offbeat and the Rock N' Roll.

What are you trying to achieve with the blog? What sorts of things do you blog about?

Fundamentally, I blog about alternative weddings. To people that don't understand what a wedding blog is, I simply describe it as just like a wedding magazine, only online. This year I've also expanded the blog into a new section called The Green Room, where I write about running your own business.

Who are your readers? What do you think they get out of your blog?

My readers are prominently brides-to-be planning their own alternative weddings. They get ideas and inspiration for their own big days. I also attract a number of readers who work in the wedding industry themselves, who either want to attract the brides to their own companies or want to get ideas about how their can run their own businesses in a way that suits them too.

What was the 'aha' moment that made you realise that this was more than just a hobby?

Before I was doing this full-time, I worked as a producer for a shopping TV channel. A guy I worked with saw my blog and told me he thought it was not only a brilliant niche and idea, but that he thought it could certainly become something that could generate an income. I guess that was the first time I started thinking that *Rock N' Roll Bride* could become more than just a hobby.

You are clearly passionate about blogging. Why do you think small businesses should be considering it? Is blogging right for everyone?

I think it is for everyone yes. Blogging is a fantastic way to showcase who you really are and show your personality, whatever your business or background. These days, particularly with weddings, people want to know about the people behind the company, and blogging and social media is a great way to do that.

Is it possible to make money from a blog? What are the criteria before this can be taken seriously?

Of course. Advertising, Google ads, affiliate schemes, ebooks and external projects like public speaking, writing for magazines/books, etc., are all ways bloggers can make money. Once you become a strong 'internet personality' the possibilities are actually endless – it's only your imagination that stops you! There are a number of things to consider, but predominately "Does my blog get enough traffic to make taking on advertising (and the hassle that goes with it) worthwhile, for both me and the potential advertisers?" i.e. does your blog get enough traffic to give them a return on their investment?

How should someone get started – practically speaking?

There are many platforms available and most are free to begin with. I would always recommend WordPress, because it's simple and very easily customisable in terms of the look of the blog.

What are your top tips for people starting blogging?

- Post regularly. I make sure I post three times a day – it's important to keep your readers happy and make sure they keep coming back to the site.

- Create a visible brand for your blog. I paid for a professional graphic designer to design my website so it looks as glossy and professional as possible.

- Don't be afraid to take risks. I gave up a day job I loved, but the risk paid off.

- Be yourself and don't follow the crowd. Don't be afraid to stand out and be different. Just be you, everyone else is taken.

Finally, what's next for Rock N' Roll Bride?

Wow, so much! A lot of the things I'm working on are top secret of course, but this year I'm planning more trips to the States for conferences and photo shoots. I started my own quarterly print magazine at the end of last year so I'll be continuing to do that, and I'm taking my 'School of Rock' blogging workshops on a tour around the UK. I've also just been asked by bridal designer Ian Stuart to model a dress he's designing especially for me, down the catwalk at The White Gallery (the bridal equivalent of Fashion Week) in May!

Quick summary

- Great quality content is 'king' online. Invest the necessary time and resources in making sure your content is exemplary.

- Search engines love blogs. And businesses with a blog do better than those without one.

- Make sure your blog posts are easily scannable to increase the chances of getting them read.

- Use blogging to personalise your brand, which will ultimately pave the way to more followers and enable you to show off your expertise. Read other blogs in your niche for fresh inspiration.

Chapter 3
Understanding Online Performance Metrics

According to Wikipedia, the free online encyclopaedia, (**en.wikipedia.org**) a key performance metric or indicator (KPI) is "an industry jargon for a type of performance measurement. KPIs are commonly used by an organization to evaluate its success or the success of a particular activity in which it is engaged."

In other words, performance metrics are the measures that help you work out how well your business is doing. To keep things simple, I will refer to performance metrics as 'performance numbers'. Which then are the performance numbers that you should look at to measure the effectiveness of your online business? Visitors? Revenue? These of course are critical variables that you will need to 'watch like a hawk' to evaluate the performance of your website and how effectively you are achieving specific improvements. Google Analytics is an excellent, free programme from Google, which will support your performance measurement efforts.

In this chapter you will learn:

- Why you should be using Google Analytics
- How to set it up
- What you should be monitoring.

Why you should be using Google Analytics

Successful businesses make effective use of feedback. Google Analytics is Google's must-have free resource to help you track your key performance indicators; your measures of how well your business is performing.

A wealth of information, all of it free, is available to all those who have a Google account and install the Google Analytics code on their sites. The service offers insights in the following ways:

1. Your visitors and their browsers

Which browsers do your visitors use? Is it Chrome or Internet Explorer? Your website's report will show a breakdown of which browsers are used and how frequently. This is useful to see, because:

(a) A significant number of visitors to your site may be coming there via a system that doesn't suit your website. You may therefore need to take action to correct any problems caused by your site not being compatible with a customer's browser. **Browsershots.org** is an excellent free resource that creates screenshots of your website design in a range of operating systems and browsers. All you do is submit your web address where indicated, and it will be added to the Browsershots job queue. When you have reached the front of the job queue, a number of distributed computers will then open up your website in their browser. These computers will generate screenshots and upload them to the Browsershots dedicated server for your review. If it is clear that your visitors are not seeing what you would ideally like them to see, you can then speak to your web designer or developer, who should be able to help you optimise your site for all browsers.

(b) Browser choice gives you an insight as to your visitor base. If it is Internet Explorer, your website has to be very easy to navigate, as the choice has indicated a basic user. If it is a newer browser, such as Chrome, a more sophisticated internet user is suggested.

2. Which content is drawing your visitors in?

Your website report will let you know which page of your website your visitors are most engaged with, and likewise, which pages they click quickly away from. Features that do not hold the interest of your visitors may not be the best investment of your small business budget, so Google Analytics has a key role to play here. The analysis will show you the top exit pages of your site, and the frequency with which your visitors navigate elsewhere. Individual pages are rated. Based on this information, you can take remedial action. On the other hand, you can act positively to further optimise any success.

3. Which keywords are important in drawing people in?

This is immensely important to your campaign. Google Analytics will report on those keywords which are the main drivers to your site. If you know which keywords are important to your visitors, you can explore advertising opportunities with sites that are complementary. You can also create additional content for those keywords and by so doing, extend your promotion.

4. How many people are simply not interested?

You need to know the numbers of those who visit, and then go away, without browsing more than just your first page. This aspect is covered by the '**Bounce rate**' feature of your Google Analytics report, which gives you a breakdown. Bounce rate is the proportion of your website's visitors who click away without attempting to go through a second, third or fourth page. Note, though, that the bounce rate will mean different things to different businesses. For example, if you want people to sign up for an email newsletter, you could get them to do just that on the first page. In that case, one page per visit won't be that bad. If on the other hand you are selling £3,000 ($4,500) bespoke, luxury holiday packages, then the more pages people look at, the more likely they are to book. You would therefore want the bounce rate to be fairly low. Ultimately, the best thing to do, whatever business you are in, is to watch your visitor numbers for major dips and peaks. Did you redesign your site, and did your bounce rate then go up drastically? Figure out why and fix it. Did you implement some changes that you thought would help but afterwards see traffic drop drastically? You can watch for those changes and adjust as quickly as possible, thanks to visitor analysis.

5. Whether your pages are 'attractive' enough to visitors

The **'Page views'** measure will show you the proportion of visitors that looks at one page, two pages, three pages, etc., on your site. If only one or two are viewed, and you are expecting much more, it might be worth considering a reorganization of content. Through spreading your main points through several pages, you draw your visitor onward and into your site.

6. What your visitors are buying

Google Analytics' Ecommerce Tracking will help you find out what visitors buy through your site, including information on:

- **Products**: The products your customers are buying, in what quantity, and the amount of money generated by those products.

- **Transactions**: The revenue, tax, shipping, and quantity information for each transaction.

- **Time to Purchase**: The number of days from the initial visit, and the total number of visits it takes for visitors to complete transactions.

With this valuable information you can gain a real understanding of:

- Which of your products sell well, and by inference, are best suited for your customer base and which ones are supported by your best promotional efforts? A product which does not sell well may not necessarily be the wrong product; rather, it may have the wrong promotion behind it.

- The revenue per sales transaction, and the number of products in each transaction. If, for example, the number of products per transaction is lower than you would ideally like, you could experiment with offering better quantity discounts, or eliminating packaging costs if customers meet a minimum amount of spend.

- How long it takes your customers to buy, and how many visits to your site it takes to encourage them to buy. So, if your sales cycles are stable, or vary predictably and regularly, e.g. seasonally, you can use this insight to make reasonably accurate predictions about your sales revenue. If customers routinely make many visits before they buy from you, it may be worth speaking to your web designer about having a site design that leads more easily to your purchase pages.

7. Whether visitors are 'mobile'

The ubiquity of smartphones and tablets requires you to keep up with that technology. If a significant portion of your website's visitors are finding you on their mobile device, which Google Analytics will show you, you will need to optimise your website for mobile technology (you should do so in any event). Mobiles could be the way a very high number of visitors are seeking you out. If so, it could be worth exploring, and then speaking to your web developer about building sites specifically designed for smartphone use. (More on optimising for mobile use is discussed in Chapter 9.)

8. When you've hit a milestone

The attention you receive is vital to your marketing. From numbers of clicks and visitors, to increases and decreases in traffic, the **'Alerts'** feature of Google Analytics can provide you with instant updates, letting you know when you've achieved milestone targets. Whether you have finally reached that million-visitor mark, or have realised you're in the danger zone as the number of first time visitors to your site (called unique visitors) has dropped by half, this function will provide the immediate information.

How to set up Google Analytics

The first login to your Google Analytics account can be a little daunting. As you have seen from the section above, there are many aspects to it. The decision as to which ones to concentrate on can be tricky, especially when you are a 'newbie' small business. In this section, I will walk you through the performance numbers (metrics) you need to watch. Before we move on however, a brief recap of the main points we have covered is needed, to refresh them in your mind.

A key performance indicator (KPI) is a measure which will help you work out how well your website is achieving your objectives. Furthermore, changes in your KPIs tell you when you need to take action.

Google Analytics will give you valuable insights into:

- Your visitors and their browsers.
- The content drawing your visitors to your site.
- The keywords drawing your visitors to your site.
- The number of people who are simply 'not interested'.

- Whether your pages are attractive enough to your visitors.
- What your visitors are buying.
- Whether your visitors are mobile.
- When you've hit a milestone.

These are in addition to those which I have already discussed in the previous chapter.

Now, let's get you set up and ready to use Google Analytics' main features.

Go to **www.google.com/analytics** and click on the 'Create an account' button.

Click on the **'Create an account'** button.

The next screen will request some basic details from you, as shown below:

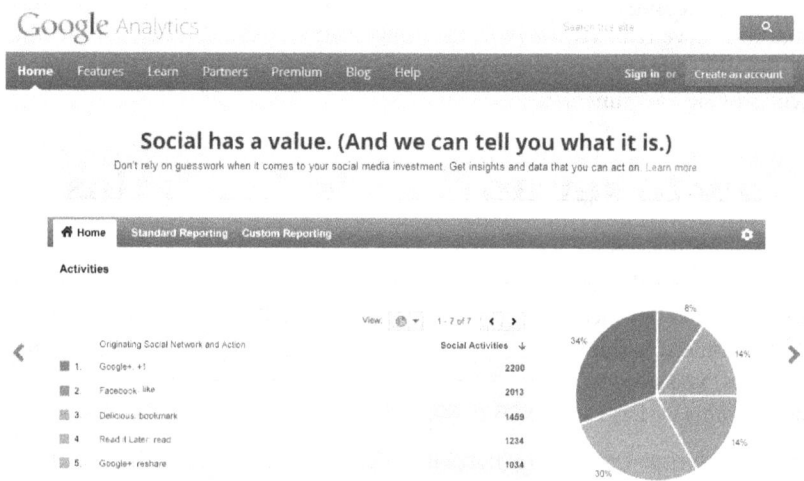

You will be asked to agree to the terms of service. Once you have done so, hit the **'Create account'** button.

After that you will be taken to a screen which lets you know that you do not currently have Google Analytics tracking on your website.

On the same screen you will be given a code to be copied and pasted onto your site – you are also given the option to email the code. This is useful if you have someone who is authorised to make changes on your site.

---

2. Paste this code on your site

Copy the following code, then paste it onto every page you want to track immediately before the closing </head> tag ?

```
<script type="text/javascript">

var _gaq = _gaq || [];
_gaq.push(['_setAccount', 'UA-34137549-1']);
_gaq.push(['_trackPageview']);

(function() {
  var ga = document.createElement('script'); ga.type = 'text/javascript'; ga.async = true;
  ga.src = ('https:' == document.location.protocol ? 'https://ssl' : 'http://www') + '.google-analytics.com/ga.js';
  var s = document.getElementsByTagName('script')[0]; s.parentNode.insertBefore(ga, s);
})();

</script>
```

› **Email these instructions** Optional

If you have a WordPress blog, you will need to click '**Appearance/Editor**' and scroll down to look for your footer.php. file on the right hand side of your screen. If you do not have a WordPress blog and you are unsure of where the code needs to go, again speak to your web designer or developer, who should be able to help you with this small task.

```
WhiteHousePro: Footer (footer.php)                    Select theme to edit:  WhiteHousePro      [▾] Select

        <div id="subfoot">                                                           Templates
            <?php if(pagelines('no_credit') || !VDEV):?>                              404 Template
                    <div id="cred" class="pagelines">                                  (404.php)
                            <a class="plimage" target="_blank" href="<?php e_pagelines('partner_link',   Carousel Page - Full Width Page
pagelines('credlink'));?>">                                                            Template
                                    <img src="<?php echo THEME_IMAGES.'/pagelines.png';?>" alt="<?php      (page-carouse-full.php)
echo THEMENAME;?> by PageLines" />                                                     Carousel Page - Standard Page
                            </a>                                                       Template
                    </div>                                                             (page-carouse.php)
            <?php endif;?>                                                             Comments
            <hr class="hidden" />                                                      (comments.php)
        </div><!--/subfoot -->                                                         Copy of header.php
                                                                                       (Copy of header.php)
    </div><!--/wrapper -->                                                             Copy of index.php
</div> <!-- end #site -->                                                              (Copy of index.php)
                                                                                       Copy of register.php
<!-- Footer Scripts Go Here -->                                                        (Copy of register.php)
        <?php if (pagelines('footerscripts')) echo pagelines('footerscripts');?>      Feature Page - Page Content
<!-- End Footer scripts -->                                                            Page Template
<?php wp_footer(); ?>                                                                  (page-feature-page.php)
                                                                                       Feature Page - Standard Page
                                                                                       Template
                                                                                       (page-feature.php)
</body>                                                                                 Footer
</html>                                                                                 (footer.php)
```

```
        </div><!--/subfoot -->

  </div><!--/wrapper -->
</div> <!-- end #site -->

<!-- Footer Scripts Go Here -->
        <?php if (pagelines('footerscri
<!-- End Footer scripts -->
<?php wp_footer(); ?>

    the code goes here!

</body>
</html>
```

I suggest pasting the code in the footer of your WordPress theme file, not in the </head>. The footer is the most common location for it. You should not have any problems in doing so.

Open up this footer.php file, and paste the code right before this code :</body>

Note: There are some theme files which allow only the Google Analytics ID. This is a code with two letters followed by a series of numbers, e.g. UA-27828853-1. If your theme has this function, then just add the Google Analytics ID, also displayed in your code.

Click '**Update File**'.

Go back to Google Analytics and hit the '**Save and Finish**' button.

After a few days, check to see the report by clicking the '**View Report**' link.

What should you be monitoring?

Ultimately, you are the only one who can really decide which are the important performance numbers (KPIs) of your business. Some websites will not do any selling, but will send traffic to other sites, for instance, or they will collect subscriptions or email sign-ups as a form of conversion. Some websites will collect money, but this might be just a small portion of their business.

So where do you start? How do you put it all together and come up with really useful data from your Analytics account?

The first thing I would recommend is for you to simply have a browse on your own to see what is there. If you are a visual person, it would also be worth you going onto YouTube and searching for 'How to use Google Analytics' or something similar. Once you feel a little more comfortable with Google Analytics and have reassured yourself that it actually is quite straightforward, here are four key foundational aspects to track:

- Visitors
- Traffic Sources Overview report
- Landing pages
- Conversions.

Visitors

Your aim is to understand how your website is being used and, using that knowledge-base, make it better. Your visitors are where you start from. If you know who is coming onto your site and for how long, you have insight into improving your subscription or your check-out process. You are also informed by the amount of time given to each page, and by the numbers of pages they look at before they leave or buy.

Your report will give you the following information:

- The total number of visits to your site.
- The number of unique visitors.
- The number of page views.
- The number of pages per visit.
- The average time on the site.
- The percentage bounce rate.
- The percentage of new visits.

Traffic sources overview report

A good starting point will be to find out how people find your website. Begin with the Traffic Sources Overview report. A healthy balance of people visiting your website by finding it through a search, arriving at it by a referral and going direct to your site is a good aim for a business; no single source should dominate traffic source distribution.

This is a pragmatic view. If you have mostly (e.g. 80%) organic search (or paid search) traffic and the mighty Google decides to make an algorithm change, it could create difficulties for your website and you would probably lose money very fast.

What does all this mean? Well, search engine rankings are not static. In other words, just because your keywords, 'gourmet chocolates' for example, are top of the results page, this is no guarantee of the same high position for ever. Businesses naturally get concerned about this because the amount of visiting traffic you get from a search engine like Google will be affected if your previous high ranking disappears. Why? Let me expand here a little. Google has a 'secret formula' (algorithm) that it uses to determine the exact positioning of websites. So, if you are ranking in first position for 'gourmet chocolates' in the spring, you could well be at bottom position for 'gourmet chocolates' in the winter, even if you have not done anything of substance to your website. Unfair? Well, it depends. I know of several businesses who have benefited from the changes to the formula and have seen their rankings improve. I also know of many businesses, including major corporations, who have been negatively impacted by the formula changes. The point is that there is very little you can do about it; as I mentioned it is a secret formula. This formula, incidentally, is also updated by Google over 500 times a year. Whilst most of these changes are minor, some modifications can be drastic and really affect how your website is ranked. Why does Google do this? Google's aim is to penalise low value content websites (sometimes called "content farms") in favour of high value, relevant websites and it uses its own complex algorithm as a means of achieving this noble aim.

If your traffic sources are more balanced and the same algorithm change affects traffic, your business should experience less of a negative impact.

Note: A new website might see most of the traffic come from a brand search, paid advertising or the direct typing-in of the website's URL.

Traffic sources are helpfully presented to you in the form of a pie chart, split into the three main traffic sources:

- Organic (search) Traffic
- Referral Traffic
- Direct Traffic.

1. Organic (search) traffic

As you implement the changes necessary to give your keywords the best position in the search rankings (which you will read about in the next chapter), you will see 'organic traffic' increasing. Organic traffic, is traffic (i.e. visitors to your site) generated by people searching for what you have via the search engines; these are people who have typed in the keywords relevant to your business, found your link and clicked through to your site. Organic traffic is free traffic, so for a small business this is clearly a good thing. You want to see a consistent and steady growth in overall traffic from natural search. (To look at the trend, go to '**Traffic Sources > Search Engines**' and you will see a graph showing your trend.) Much of your work as a small business internet entrepreneur will be to try to increase this part, and spend less on paid advertising.

2. Referral traffic

Referral traffic is made up of visitors who come to your site from direct links on other sites, such as a link on someone else's blog. This happens if someone likes your website, products or services enough to recommend them by posting a link to your site on their blog. Referral traffic is therefore not the same as organic traffic, which is traffic from search engines, such as Google. Visitors arriving via pay per click ads, which I cover later in this book, also constitute referral traffic.

Referral traffic can be extremely useful:

- If the traffic source is another blog. In this situation you can build a relationship with the other site, or blogger, for example by leaving pithy or just helpful comments for them on their blog.

- If the source is a search engine, you can consider creating similar content.

- If you can see that the source is one of the social media platforms. In this case, you must get more active in that network, and if you haven't already done so, place sharing buttons on your site (as shown below), and educate your current readers about how to use them.

How to place social-sharing buttons on your site

- Go to **share.lockerz.com/buttons** to find a screen similar to the one below (it may have been tweaked by the time you are reading this).

Grab the button

Type	Share/Bookmark Widget ▾
Button	⦿ 🔖 Share / Save 🖪 🖐 🖪 ▾ ○ 🔖 Share / Save ▾ More » ○ ➕ Share │ 🖪 🖐 ✉
Email address	Optional (for updates)

Get Button Code   More Options »

Copy and paste this into your page:

🔖 Share / Save 🖪 🖐 🖪 ▾

```
<!-- Lockerz Share BEGIN -->
<a class="a2a_dd" href="http://www.addtoany.com/share_save"><
<script type="text/javascript" src="http://static.addtoany.co
<!-- Lockerz Share END -->
```

- Ensure you have selected the **'Share/Bookmark Widget'** option and selected the button of your choice.

- Click on the **'Get Button Code'** link – you do not have to enter your email address.

- If you feel confident to do so, copy and paste the code given onto the page of your website where you want the button to appear. If you do not feel confident enough to do so, ask your website developer or designer for help – it only takes a few minutes.

- If you have a WordPress blog, you can download the sharing button from here: **wordpress.org/extend/plugins/add-to-any/installation**. Ask your website developer to upload the button into the **'Plug-ins directory'** of your blog and then activate it through the **'Plug-ins menu'**, which is in your WordPress dashboard. Once activated, you and your website developer can control the location of the sharing button by going to the **'Settings menu'** in your dashboard. For example, you can choose whether to have the button at the top or bottom of blog posts.

Whatever the referral source, you can look at the content that's working out and produce more of it.

3. Direct Traffic

With this form of traffic, people have arrived at your site directly by either typing in your website address (your URL) or via a bookmark. Hence, direct traffic is not traffic that results from people clicking on links on other sites to your site (that's referral traffic), it is not traffic that comes to your site by clicking on ads (that's 'Other' in Google Analytics), it is not people who come from search engines (that is search/organic traffic or pay per click advertising traffic – such as the links you see on the right hand side of the search results). Direct traffic visitors are one of the most important types of visitor your website could get. To have specifically chosen to visit your website, it is the most targeted type of website traffic. Direct traffic visitors are also not affected by outside factors, such as when there are changes in search engine rankings, which I touched on earlier.

Tips for increasing your direct traffic:

- Have a memorable website address (and website, too!).

- Ensure all your stationery – business cards, letterheads, etc., and your email signature clearly has your website address on them. Include your website details in any form that asks for your contact information.

- Make your site an authority on your niche by having up to date, regularly updated, high quality content. Aim to become the go-to website in your niche.

- Make sure your existing customers, past purchasers and suppliers all have your website details – give them a good reason to go onto your site.

- At networking and industry events, always make sure you have your business cards with you, with your website address on them.

- If you do any offline advertising, e.g. in newspapers or magazines, make sure your website address is included in the copy.

- Family and friends are an underused asset! Make sure they have a stock of business cards with your web address printed on, so they can hand them out too.

If you look at the individual source reports, you can see 'All Traffic', 'Direct Referrals', 'Search' and 'Campaigns'.

'Campaigns' is where your PPC, or pay per click, accounts should live (visit the Google Analytics Help page for a visual how-to on this). With this in mind, there is a third, important element of your internet marketing to track: landing page metrics.

Landing pages

Landing pages and their role in advertising is discussed more fully in Chapter 5, but a definition now will further support your understanding later on. At its simplest, a landing page is any web page that a visitor can 'land' on. They are stand alone web pages that are distinct from your main website and which have been designed for a single focused objective.

Because landing pages are stand alone, there need not be any global navigation to tie them to your primary or main website. This is to limit the options presented to your visitors and encourage them towards your intended sales objective; your 'conversion goal'.

There are two main types of landing page: Click-through and Lead Generation. Click-through landing pages are geared towards persuading a visitor to 'click through' to another page. These pages are commonly used by ecommerce businesses. How it works is that a product or offer is described in just enough detail to entice a visitor to the point whereby they are close to making a buying decision. Generally speaking, most advertising campaigns are geared towards sending a visitor to the shopping cart pages. This tends to lead to disappointing results when not enough visitors buy – understandably, as most of us prefer to make an informed decision before buying and there usually isn't enough information in these advertisements. With a click-through landing page, the destination page after the landing page is the shopping cart page. This results in a greater chance of conversion, as the visitor will have willingly entered their details on the landing page first. It is the extra step that makes the difference.

Lead generation landing pages are designed primarily to capture visitor contact information, such as name, address and telephone number. This will allow a business to market to that visitor at a later date. To that end, a lead generation page will contain a form with a description of an offer given in return for submitting the personal contact information. There are many uses for lead generation landing pages such as:

- Consultation for professional services
- Discount coupon/voucher
- Free trial, e.g. a 30 day free trial
- A physical gift (via direct mail)
- Notification of a future product launch.

The length of a lead generation form and the amount of data requested can affect conversions, so beware of asking for too much information. Instead, ask for the minimum amount of information that you need to be able to market to your prospective customers effectively.

Analysing performance numbers on your landing pages (we discuss landing pages and their role in advertising in Chapter 5) is important in understanding whether the information you are delivering matches the needs of the traffic you are getting. What should you measure though? Here are three important performance numbers you need to watch:

1. Conversion rate: Your conversion rate is a ratio of prospects to completed transactions. How you define a completed transaction will be specific to your business. Many companies use the internet purely to generate leads. In this case, what is of interest to them is a completed lead form.

Most businesses will actually be interested in measuring, calculating, and improving several different conversion rates. Fortunately, it is not difficult to calculate your conversion rate. Use this simple formula:

Total conversions ÷ Total views x 100 = Conversion rate (%)

Here are some examples of how you could compute conversion rates for different scenarios and transaction types:

Lead Generation Conversion Rate: *Number of lead forms filled out ÷ Traffic on landing page x 100 = Conversion rate (%)*

Website Lead Conversion Rate: *Number of lead forms filled out ÷ Total traffic on home page x 100 = Conversion rate (%)*

Website Sales Conversion Rate: *Number of sales ÷ Number of visitors x 100 = Conversion rate (%)*

2. Abandonment rate: The percentage of people who looked at your landing page, but didn't complete it.

You can calculate your abandonment rate for a form by comparing the number of views of the form with the number of views of the Thank You page, or whatever page it is your visitor lands on after they press your 'Submit', or similar, button. If you have no discrete, measurable page which is served when someone fills in a form, then speak to your landing page designer and ask them to change the design, so as you have something to measure.

The basic rule for reducing abandonment on forms is to ask fewer questions of your visitors. Many businesses treat lead capture forms as an opportunity to engage in some market research. They may ask questions like "How much is your budget?" or "Where did you find our site?" Each of these questions – usually unnecessary from the customer's viewpoint – is a reason for someone not to complete the forms. Remember what your landing page form is for – to get the minimum contact information from a potential customer so as you can sell to them.

3. Cost per action: This calculation will tell you how much you need to spend to get a sale. You can measure your cost per action, or cost per sale, by dividing your advertising costs by the amount of sales in a given time period to come up with the average cost that you spend on getting one sale. There are some online tools that will calculate your cost per action for you, such as this one from Clickz (**www.clickz.com/cpa-calculator**).

Note that high abandonment on paid advertising to landing pages means that you need to improve that experience for the user. Below are suggestions of what you could consider to improve your landing page:

- Your headline. This should be a clear expression of your value proposition; the value of your offering to your visitors.
- Your content. A landing page should have a single focus and therefore single message. Edit to remove unnecessary content. Be succinct.
- Simplify your copy using bullets.
- Provide a guarantee to either remove or reduce risk.
- Use testimonials from people with real names.
- Your call to action (CTA) – specifically, the text on your 'Click here if you want xx' button.
- Images. Try a variation of your main photo – for example, a photo that shows your product or service being used.
- Consider using video, which is consumed avidly online.
- Button design. Accentuate the look of your CTA (use contrast, whitespace, different – preferably larger – sizes).

- Form length. Try to minimise the amount of fields that visitors are required to complete and go for the minimum amount of information you need.

- Long copy vs. short copy. As a general rule the shorter the better, although for some products the detail is important, e.g. software products.

- It is also a good idea to look at sending your PPC, email, social media, organic and banner advertising traffic to landing pages. This will help you to see which channel performs best. (Banner adverts are image or text-only adverts that appear on websites; they come in different sizes and are measured in pixels – for more on banner advertising visit **marketing.yell.com/web-design/what-is-banner-advertising**).

Conversions

If you are collecting money from your website then you will need to track your conversions from the beginning. It can be tricky to do this, so in the interest of doing it properly, I would suggest finding an expert who can set it up and configure it for you. If you do choose to do it yourself, Google has a how-to on configuring ecommerce tracking:
support.google.com/analytics/bin/answer.py?hl=en&answer=1009612

Quick summary

It is difficult, if not impossible, to measure your progress if you do not know what to measure or how to measure it. The four key reports: visitors, traffic sources overview, landing pages and conversion tracking, will give you the vital information you need to critically analyse your progress and make the necessary changes in your internet marketing campaigns.

Chapter 4
How to Get Found Online Through Search Engine Optimisation (SEO)

This chapter includes:

- How to implement a keyword strategy.
- How to make your website visible through search engine optimisation, tags, metadata and links (for technophobes).
- Submitting an XML sitemap.
- How to optimise for local search and rank high in your local market – local SEO.
- Expert interview – SEO
- Getting listed in product directories.

Keywords

Keywords are the phrases used by people searching on search engines for information, products or services. As an example of a possible product, I shall use vermeil jewellery.

Keywords also help search engines, such as Google, determine if your website pages are relevant to the search terms that are entered by a searcher.

In this section we will look at how you can start to implement a keyword strategy for your business. In particular, we will look at how you can:

- Determine keywords for your business.
- Use the free Google Keyword tool.
- Sift for the best keywords.

How to implement your keyword strategy

The first thing to do here is to perform a keyword analysis – a check of the keywords that people use when they are searching for your product or service. The following are some steps you can take to get you started:

1. Identify the obvious phrases. Open a Word document and simply type all the words that come to mind regarding your business offering (e.g. vermeil jewellery would include rings, necklaces, charms, etc.). If geography is important then include terms that involve your town/city or nearby cities.

2. When brainstorming your keywords, it is a very good idea to include synonyms as well – it may be worth using a Thesaurus. Why is this important? Consider the word 'house'. Whilst this is the more commonly used term in English speaking countries, Americans tend to use the term 'home' more routinely. It is also worth going through your list and adding singulars and plurals. Search engines treat singulars and plurals differently. For example, a search on the word 'book' will generate a different search volume to 'books' and it will be important to know which is searched for the most.

3. Similarly, consider your keywords that can either be searched for as two separate words or as one word, e.g. roundup, round up. Consider common spelling mistakes – many words are often misspelled when typed into search engines; for example stationery, calendar, and jewellery. If the traffic from a misspelling is very significant, you may want to create a page that is optimised for the misspelt version. A good tip is to include the various constructions of the word inside your TITLE tags, which I discuss below. Optimising in this way for misspelt words can be good for 'free 'n' easy' traffic that chooses you in preference to competitors, who may not be quite as savvy as you.

4. Likewise, if there are any hyphenated words on your list that could be used without the hyphen, add both versions to your list and have a look

to see which of the versions is more common. Search engines treat them as different searches; common examples are ecommerce and e-commerce, or email and e-mail.

Title tags

Title tags, for example <TITLE>calendar, calendar?</TITLE> are essentially pieces of HTML code that describe a specific web page's content through a keyword query that a person types into a search engine. Title tags are a very important guide for all search engines in determining what is in the content of a specific web page. Creating a relevant title tag is one of the most important variables in achieving high search engine positioning. You should consider your Title Tag as a representation of your core keywords of the most important services and offerings. Unfortunately, title tags are often wasted because so many sites don't bother placing in useful keywords. The titles are usually generic: Welcome to Our Lovely Company, or Lovely Company Inc – Home Page. These titles are not beneficial for getting your keywords in the best possible position in the search engine results page. Give the search engines a really strong clue about what your website is all about by using a relevant keyword phrase in the title tag.

Here is an example of how a Title Tag is placed within the website coding from **seomoz.org**:

```
<!DOCTYPE html>
<html>
<head>
    <meta http-equiv="X-UA-Compatible" content="IE=Edge"/>
    <title>Search seomoz</title>
```

You can view the title tag of a website by going to '**View**' on the toolbar and then '**Source**'. A website title is important because search engines use website titles to scan sites for search results. The title tag is best defined as a description of a webpage's content. This description should not be longer than 70 characters as this is the limit Google displays in search results. The description of the page needs to be inserted between two tags, shown in the screenshot above as <title> and </title>. Changing the TITLE tag on a WordPress blog is straightforward, however if you do not have a WordPress blog and you wish to change the title tags of your website, a web developer will need to edit the HTML code of your website and then replace the website code with the edited version of the HTML.

Title tags appear in the search results as shown here:

Google Analytics, which I discussed in the previous chapter, is your key tool to discovering the keywords people are using to come to your site. Locate the keywords in the tool and add them to your Word document list of keywords.

Spy on the competition's keyword tags. If you don't know who your competitors are, Google your business or service offering, and see which websites rank for those keywords. Then, once you have identified the top five or so, visit each one and click 'View' then 'Source' on the browser's menu bar, then look for the <META NAME= "here are the keywords"> tag for relevant keywords.

Ask business colleagues and loyal customers their opinion. Show customers and colleagues the keywords on your Word list and ask them to add any others they think are suitable.

Using the free Google Keyword tool

Go to **www.adwords.google.com/select/KeywordToolExternal**. It is important to note that Google will not show you all the results it could show you. At the time of writing though, if you sign up to an AdWords account (**www.adwords.com**), you can get access to the tool in full, i.e. all the keywords, without having to run any ads – therefore you do not need to pay a penny. When you first load the tool you will see a page that looks like the one shown in the screenshot below. There are three ways you can get started:

1.. Type a keyword into the **'Word or Phrase'** box, or type multiple phrases with each phrase on a separate line.

2. In the **'Website'** field, type in the URL of one of your main competitors. Then click the **'Find Keywords'** button.

3. Select a **'Category'** from the left-hand column.

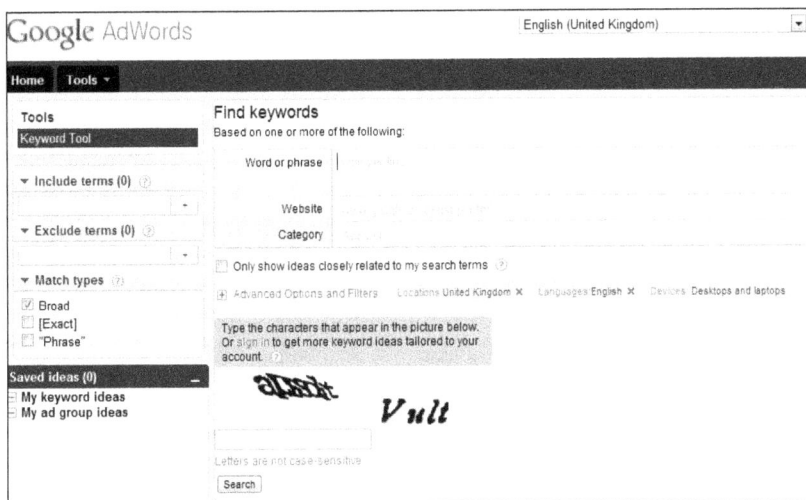

What you are doing is asking Google to look through its database of searches – the actual keywords used by searchers on its website and partner sites – to find searches that it thinks are related to your keyword phrase, the website URL you entered, or the category you picked. Other cool things you can do are:

- Limit the keywords to searches within a particular country or language.

- Limit the information only to searches carried out on mobile devices that have internet data access.

- Filter results using criteria such as 'Show low competition keywords only'.

Limit the information just to those keyword phrases that include the actual term you typed in. For the first two methods, all you do is click the **'Search'** button and Google finds keywords related to your search term. In the example below, I simply entered a search for vermeil, and Google returned the following a range of related keywords, such as gold vermeil, vermeil beads and vermeil bracelet.

Keyword	Competition	Global Monthly Searches	Local Monthly Searches
vermeil ▾	Low	74,000	3,600

Keyword ideas (72)

Keyword	Competition	Global Monthly Searches	Local Monthly Searches
vermeil findings ▾	High	480	140
gold vermeil ▾	Medium	8,100	1,000
gold filled ▾	Medium	60,500	3,600
cartier vermeil ▾	High	1,900	260

If you logged in through your AdWords account first, you would have been served many more keywords. To sort your keywords, all you do is click on the column headings. In the example below, I sorted by competition through simply clicking on the competition heading:

Search Sign in with your AdWords login information to see the full set of ideas for this search.

Search Terms (1)

Keyword	▲ Competition
vermeil ▾	Low

Keyword ideas (72)

Keyword	▲ Competition
define vermeil ▾	Low
vermeil definition ▾	Low
definition of vermeil ▾	Low
vermeil gold definition ▾	Low
gold vermeil definition ▾	Low
gold filled vs vermeil ▾	Low
vermeil vs gold filled ▾	Low
gold vermeil vs gold filled ▾	Low
what is vermeil ▾	Low
gold vermeil ▾	Medium
what is vermeil gold ▾	Medium
what is gold vermeil ▾	Medium
vermeil gold ▾	Medium
yellow gold vermeil ▾	Medium

You can also add or remove columns by using the **'Views'** button on the right-hand side of the screen.

Number of searches

The number of searches you see does not accurately reflect the number of times your keywords are searched for. This is essentially an advertising tool intended to help you work with your pay per click advertising campaigns. The number of searches you see reflects the number of searches your advert would match every month if you chose to use the search term in question. So, if your keywords are vermeil gold, your advert would be matched with approximately 880 local searches per month. When you advertise with Google's pay per click system, you have to say when your advert should run. So, for example, your advertisement could be specified to run when someone searches for vermeil or vermeil jewellery. In effect, Google is saying to you that, "When you create your ad to be triggered by a broad match of the term vermeil jewellery, your ad could be triggered up to 880 times per month".

Match types

Have a look at the left hand side of the AdWords tool. There you will see a section entitled **'Match Type'**. This determines how an advert will be matched with a search term.

Broad: This is the default match type. Google will return an advert that is similar to, or a relevant variation of, the keyword that is searched for. The downside of broad matches is that the advert can be triggered by many different searches, so, for example, if an advertisment was triggered by a broad match of vermeil jewellery, then it could also be triggered by jewellery, precious stones, etc.

Exact: With this, a keyword phrase will trigger an advert only if the exact phrase is searched for. For example, if an advert is triggered by the keywords vermeil jewellery, using an exact match, the advert will only be served when someone searches for the exact phrase vermeil jewellery.

Phrase: With this type of match, an advertisment is served when someone searches either for the exact phrase, or for the exact phrase in combination with other words. If, for example, an advert is set to come up on the phrase vermeil jewellery to a phrase match, the advert could be triggered when someone searches for cheap vermeil jewellery.

How many searches?

I would suggest discarding any keywords that have a low number (e.g. 800) of monthly searches. Equally, it is important to avoid very generic keywords that have a huge monthly traffic. Whilst such a quantity will not cost you anything financially, it does signal huge competition and makes it much harder to rank near the top of the search engines.

Tip

Remember to include the word 'buy' alongside your product names in your copy as much as possible, as many searches will type 'buy vermeil jewellery' rather than just 'vermeil jewellery'. Similarly, if your product is seasonal, include 'spring' or 'Christmas' in your copy alongside it.

Useful resources

Keyword Spy (**www.keywordspy.com**) is a great competitive intelligence tool, as it lets you see which keywords your competitors are spending money on in their advertising campaigns. There is also historical data that lets you see how keyword use may have changed over time.

Making your site visible – SEO, tags, metadata, and links

SEO (Search Engine Optimisation)

Search engines such as Google will reward your content's 'relevance' to keywords that are searched for. What this really means is that if searchers enter 'gourmet chocolates' into the search box, and they are served a link to your website, on clicking on that link they will find information about gourmet chocolates. In other words, your content will be relevant to their search needs. Your aim as a business on the web is to make sure that the right pages from your site appear as high up as possible in the search engine result rankings. The process of achieving this is referred to as search engine optimisation, or SEO. Why bother? Well, to start with, the overwhelming majority of searchers do not go beyond the first page and again, the overwhelming majority of searchers (more than 90% of them) will not look beyond where their eye can see without the need to scroll down (also referred to as below the fold). Good search engine optimisation involves ensuring not only that you get your content right, but also that you structure your content in such a way that the best possible position in the search results for your website is achieved.

Search engines will serve up a link to an entire page. What you have on your pages, therefore, is pretty important to them. Generally speaking, you should ensure that each page deals with a single major content piece. If you have a variety of products, each should ideally have its own dedicated page. If, for example, you have both vermeil and silver ranges of jewellery, each needs to be on its own page. This way, the density of the relevant keywords on the page is much higher.

In this section we'll have a quick look at the main elements important in getting your website fit for search engine optimisation purposes.

Structure

Your content needs to be structured in such a way that it emphasises the main messages within it. Google tends to give extra value to the top 25% and the bottom 25% of content on any page. When it comes to deciding if a page is relevant, the keywords in those places will outrank those that are in the main, middle part of the copy. Ergo, place your important messages and keywords near the top and the bottom.

HTML tags

Before you get scared off, remember that this guide is for technophobes; no particularly advanced HTML knowledge is needed. I am most certainly not an HTML expert – I know enough to get my website where it needs to be – no more, no less! So, let's look at the tags you do need to have an appreciation of. I suggest you discuss these with your web designer and ensure that the tags have been configured as described in the following sections.

Header tags

The most important HTML tag to have an understanding of is the <h1> header tag. **H1 or <h1> tags** can improve your search engine ranking. But maybe you don't know what that means, or even how to tell if your website is using the <h1>

tag properly to maximise your search engine placement. Think of these tags as 'heading tags'. Online, headings are pieces of coding that allow you to make certain words (i.e. your most important keywords) stand out on a page. To understand how headings work on a web page, consider an article in a magazine. The title of the article will stand out from the rest of the copy. It will usually be formatted in bold, with a different font or colour to make it more pronounced than the rest of the content of the page. An <h1> tag is similar. It allows you to emphasise certain words, which allows readers of your website to see quickly what the page is all about and decide whether or not to carry on reading. The H1 tag is the most important heading, because it's the highest level tag that shows what your specific page is about. Search engines generally give this tag more weight over other headings, so it usually improves your search engine ranking when you use it correctly and in conjunction with the other techniques discussed in this chapter. There are other headings which are important too. These are the <h2>, <h3>, <h4>, etc. tags that are usually used as sub-headings and should help you organise your content so it is easier to read. They do not carry as much weight as the<h1> tags where search engines are concerned. However they should also contain important keywords.

To see if your pages are using <h1> tags, follow these steps:

1. Open your internet browser and go to the website address (the URL) of the page you want to check.

2. Click **'View'**, then **'Source'**. A new window will open displaying the HTML code.

3. Click **'Edit'**, then **'Find'**.

4. Type in <h1> and click **'Find Next'**.

5. This will now highlight the sections of your site that are using the H1 tag.

6. Follow the same steps for H2, H3, H4, H5 and H6.

To determine if you're putting your H1 tag to good use, follow this advice (or ask your web developer to assist you):

- Your website should have only one H1 tag. If you have more than one H1 tag on a page, change the other H1 tags to an H2 or H3.

- Your H1 tag should contain your most important keywords for that page and if possible the first word or words in the H1 should be the keywords. These should also match the page title keywords and META keywords.

- Your H1 tag should help your reader understand what the page is about.

Image tags and ALT attributes

<IMG> or image tags are used to insert images into web pages. These tags can also use what is called the ALT= attribute, which means alternative text. ALT text was originally shown if the browser viewing the web page could not display images. ALT text is also used by programmes that 'speak' the page for those people who may be visually impaired. In many browsers the ALT text also appears in a little pop-up box when you hold your mouse over an image for a few moments. Incidentally, if you have a Firefox browser you can install an add-on called Popup ALT Attribute to make this happen.

ALT attributes are read by search engines. This is because these tag 'attributes' offer another clue about the content of the page. For this reason it is important to place keywords in your ALT attributes. If you are not confident enough to do this yourself, I suggest you assign this task to your web developer or designer, who should be able to help you initially.

Keywords can be placed in your ALT attributes like this: <IMG SRC= London-gourmet-chocolates-1.jpg" ALT= "London gourmet chocolates – chocolate gifts-chocolate hampers"/>

Use these ALT attributes on image links, as doing so will give the search engines an idea of what the page referenced by the link is all about. To learn more about inserting image tags and other tags, I highly suggest this website (**www.w3schools.com/tags/tag_img.asp**) to support your understanding of using tags. You can also can try your hand at working with tags on the site too.

Metadata and Tags

Metadata, which is worth paying attention to, is the "Description" Meta tag. Why? Simply, this is the tag that helps you control how your site appears in the search results. All the main search engines use this tag as the text that appears beneath the site link. Google and Bing use the text on its own. Yahoo! however will pad it out with content from your site to fill the available space. In the absence of a Description Meta Tag, the search engines will simply grab some content from your page and present that, giving you no control over what appears.

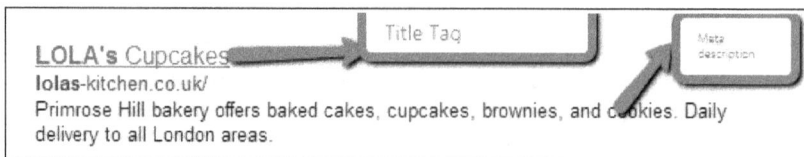

LOLA's Cupcakes — Title Tag
lolas-kitchen.co.uk/
Primrose Hill bakery offers baked cakes, cupcakes, brownies, and cookies. Daily delivery to all London areas. — Meta description

Title Tags

I have already introduced the title tags to you ealier on in this chapter. In this section I will return to them in a little more detail. The title tag is the single most important tag on your webpage. The title tag is used to declare the title of your webpage, and it appears not only on your page but also at the top of the web browser screen when that page is viewed (or in a tab in some browsers, such as Google Chrome) and in a visitor's bookmarks menu, if the page is bookmarked as shown below:

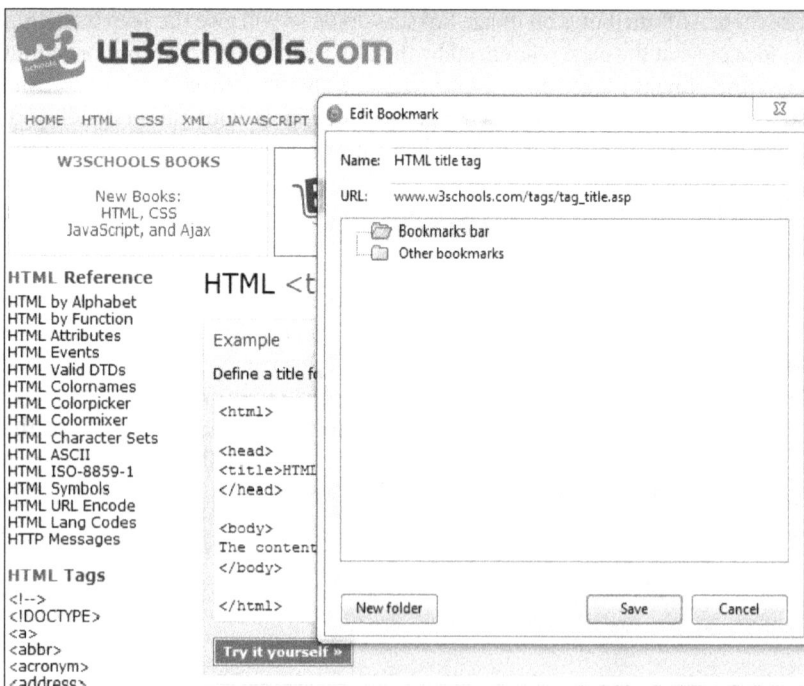

Search engines use titles to index websites, and often display them in search engine results. A page title should be no more than 70 characters.

If you have a WordPress blog, creating and editing page titles couldn't be easier. Simply locate **'Pages'** in your dashboard menu, and click **'Add new'**. In the box that appears, enter the title you want for your page. To delete or edit a page title, simply go to **'Pages'**, locate the page you want to edit or trash and then perform the desired action.

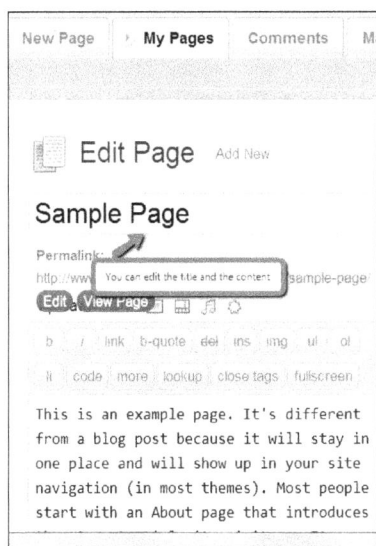

WordPress will use the page title you enter in the title box you are presented with in three different ways: it will appear as the name of the page, the title in the browser and also as the opening headline.

Most search engines will use the site's <TITLE> tag as the link and main title of the site's listing on the search results page. These tags instruct a browser as to which text should show up in the browser's title bar and are very important for search engines too. Search engine spiders (programmes that crawl over the web for the purpose of 'feeding' pages to search engines) will read page titles and use that information to determine what the pages are all about. If your <TITLE> tags have a keyword within them that competing pages do not have, you have a good chance of being ranked higher in the results.

If you do not have a WordPress blog, you will need to ask your web developer to show you how to insert them correctly with the following guidelines in mind:

- **Length**: Title tags should be no more than 70 characters long, including spaces.

- **Keyword Placement**: Your most important words (keywords) need to be first in your title tag.

- **Keyword Separation**: Use pipes | to separate important keyword phrases. Do not use commas, underscores, dashes or any other punctuation unless the keyword is written that way.

- **Use of words**: Omit filler words, such as 'and', 'if', 'but', 'then', etc.

- **Company Name**: If your company name is not part of the important (keyword) phrases, put it at the end of the title tag.

- **Unique**: Title tags must be unique, i.e. one title tag for each page.

- **Relevance**: Title tags should be descriptive of the content on the page, e.g. the About Page would be: About | Important Keywords | Company Name or Important Keywords | About Us | Company Name [if not mentioned previously].

Keyword 'Stuffed' Title Tags

I have come across some websites with inappropriately written title tags. Usually, these are sites that want to rank highly for every single keyword that applies to their business and what they will do is repeat the word within the title tags. This practice is one which is very much frowned upon by search engines; you have been warned!

Imagine you wanted to rank for blue doors and green doors. If you were practicing keyword 'stuffing' your title tag would appear similar to this:

> **Blue doors, green doors, every possible colour of door | doors doors and even more doors| Doors.com**

Hopefully I do not need to tell you that this does not look good. A better effort would be:

> **Blue & green doors | coloured doors | Doors.com**

I have removed the unnecessary repetition and filler words such as 'and', replacing the latter with an ampersand (&) and have combined the products (you could equally split these products to separate pages – one for blue doors and one for green doors – however, this isn't always feasible or desirable). I have also added a category keyword which would appear in the middle of the title tag on all coloured doors related page titles, then end it with the domain name for branding purposes.

Some Title Tag Writing Examples

If your important words (keywords) were 'Usain Bolt' and 'Winning' your title tag would be written in that order:

Usain Bolt Winning

Usain Bolt would be the first words in the tag.

What if your keywords were 'Usain Bolt Winning' and 'Sportswear'? Your title tag would still be written with 'Usain Bolt Winning' as the first words in the tag. Then you would add a pipe | and 'Sportswear' as the second phrase:

Usain Bolt Winning | Sportswear

Avoid using hyphens, underscores, commas or any other type of character – stick to the pipes shown.

If you wanted to add your company name, 'Amy's Place', you would do so as shown to 'Usain Bolt Winning' and 'Sportswear' and 'Amy's Place'; you would separate these three phrases with pipes, with 'Amy's Place' last and farthest from the beginning, which Google sees as the least important phrase:

Usain Bolt Winning | Sportswear | Amy's Place

Tip

- To learn more about writing tags, visit the support blog **www.seomoz.org/learn-seo/title-tag**.

- If you would prefer to watch a video about title tags, visit YouTube (**www.youtube.com/watch?v=R7hrPLAmbao**) where you will find several mini-tutorials on writing and editing these tags.

Links

Links in your web pages have several very important functions, including the following:

- They help the search engine spiders find other pages in your site.
- Keywords in links tell search engines about the pages that the links are pointing at.
- Keywords within links tell search engines about the page that has the links.

There are three kinds of links that you will need for your site to be successful:

1. Links within your site
2. Incoming links
3. Outgoing links.

1. Links within your site

When you are creating your pages, create links on the page to other pages, and also ensure that other pages within your site link back to the page you are creating – using the keywords you placed in your <TITLE>tag.

Create 'anchor text' links with your keywords in them. For example, if your keywords are 'vermeil jewellery', anchor text links would look like these with the links pointing to the appropriate destination page:

For pricing information refer to our vermeil jewellery pricing page. (Someone clicking on this link would be taken to the pricing page.)

Our vermeil jewellery range is beautifully displayed in our gallery. (Someone clicking on the link would be taken to your gallery.)

2. Incoming links

Google ranks its results on three main factors: relevance (which I have mentioned already), age (the longer-established sites tend to appear higher up the listings), and then the number and quality of links on the site. Search engines can still find out about your site however, in at least two very important ways: by having links pointing to your site and by sitemap submissions (which are discussed later on in this chapter).

Getting links pointing to your site

Your aim should be to get incoming links from authoritative sites. The best way to do this is by providing free information that is of interest to visitors. You should also register your site with search directories. The Open Directory Project (**www.dmoz.org**) is well-recognised and used by major search engines. This should be one of your first ports of call. Other directories should be chosen carefully; make sure they are relevant and have a higher Page Rank than yours.

Ways to generate links include:

- **Contacting manufacturers' websites**: If you sell products, contact the manufacturers of those products, and ask them to place a link to your website on their product page.

- **Contacting association sites**: Contact any professional or business associations of which you are a member, and ask for a link to your website to be posted – for example, through their directory of members.

- **Submitting to press release services**: Send out press releases regularly to **www.Prweb.com**

- **Contacting companies you do business with**: Ask to be placed on their list of clients.

- **Asking to be a featured client**: If you have had a favourable experience with a related company this can work well.

- **Promoting through social media**: Create and/or promote something of value that is on your site, and then spread the word through social media sites, such as Twitter or Facebook.

Don't forget offline marketing to promote incoming links. It is another way you can help your online service. Here are some examples:

- Include your website address in all printed materials – letterhead, business card, order form, brochure, fax etc., as well as in promotional tools – stickers, posters.

- Sponsor an event – an efficient way to raise your business profile.

- Go to trade shows in your niche – the opportunity here is to introduce your site to a targeted audience, network with complementary businesses and discover your competition.

- In your local area – send a press release to local newspapers and radios to show your local involvement. Put up flyers and posters in local shops.

- Contact customers and former customers so they know that you have a website available. Show them the benefits they will get if they use your website, e.g. discounted prices, online only vouchers, etc.

- Colleagues, friends, relatives – use your personal network!

3. Outgoing links

Sooner or later you will probably be asked by email to exchange links. In other words, the emailer offers to add a link to your site in return for you adding a link to theirs. As a rule of thumb, if you are offered a link exchange by a site with a higher Page Rank than yours, then I suggest that, providing the site is a relevant one, you accept.

All outgoing links should be set to launch in a "blank window page". All Web browsers feature the ability to open a new window. The option can be found in your navigation menu under "File", and then "New Window". A blank browser window will display on top of the current one.

A blank window page helps you to keep your visitor on your site, as the page you are linking to will open in a new window, without closing yours. This will prevent visitors being transported to that site, out of sight of yours. To launch a blank window for an outgoing link, follow these steps (or ask your web developer to guide you):

Log into your blog or web server and find the post in which you want to insert an outgoing link. Click on the spot on the page where you want the link to appear. If you have a WordPress blog, you will need to click in the HTML view of your page.

Type the following: <A HREF =(this indicates that you are creating a link)

Type the web address you wish to link to. For example, to link out to a page with the following address would look like this:

http://www.joba.com. Type the full URL address as shown, keeping the quotation marks intact around the URL. Press the space bar once and type "TARGET= "_blank." Once again, keep the quotation marks intact.

After typing the words "TARGET = "_blank", type immediately after this >whatever you wish goes in this space</A>. Replace my wording of "whatever you wish goes in this space" with the words you want to appear in the link itself.

Ensure your code appears exactly in this format:

<A HREF= "http://www.joba.com" TARGET= "_blank">whatever you wish goes in this space</A>.

Don't forget to replace http://www.joba.com and "whtever you wish goes in this space" with the actual web address and the link words you want to use.

Once you have written your link as shown, click "Publish".

When the blank window page opens, your site will remain as an option in the taskbar (Windows) or Mission Control (Mac). Many browsers also have "tabbed browsing" which would open that blank window in the same Web window as your site.

It is also a good idea to link out to complementary sites within your posts, perhaps to add extra value to points you have made already, and which have been made by another site. Again, link out to sites which have a higher Page Rank than yours.

Submitting an XML sitemap

XML stands for Extensible Markup Language. Submitting an XML sitemap is a very important form of site submission that can help to improve the indexing of your site. You create an XML sitemap and submit this to the top three search engines, and make it easy for other search engines, such as **www.ask.com**, to find the sitemap too.

An XML sitemap is a special file placed on your site that contains an index to help search engines find their way to your pages. You create and place the file and then let the search engines know where it is. This hidden file is in a format meant for search engines. Once you have submitted a sitemap and 'verified' your submission, the search engines also give you a good amount of information about your site!

Creating a sitemap

If you have a small site you can use sitemap generators, such as **www.xml-sitemaps.com**. You simply enter your domain name into a web page and it spiders your site, creating the sitemap as it goes along, of up to 500 pages. If your site is bigger than 500 pages, you can get the service to install a script on your web server for a small amount of money. WordPress has a free plug-in to create a sitemap automatically:

1. In your Word Press dashboard – in your Plug-ins menu, click on '**Add new**'. Next, in the search box type in '**Google xml**' followed by '**Search plugins**'.

1. In the list that you will be given, locate the Google sitemap generator from Arne Brachhold. Click '**Install**', then '**Install now**'.

2. Next, click on '**Activate plug-in**'. Then, go to your Settings menu in your dashboard and click on '**Settings/XML-Sitemap**'.

3. To generate the site map, select the '**Click here**' button to create your first sitemap.xml file for your WordPress blog. Once you click that button, you can find your site map by searching for: **www.yourdomain.com/sitemap.xml**

4. To submit your sitemap to Google, go to the Webmaster tools website via your Gmail account: Go to **www.google.com/webmasters/tools**, click the '**Add a site**' button and type the URL of your site.

1. Click '**Continue**'.

2. You will be asked to prove that the site indeed belongs to you, and will be presented with the following in the '**Alternative Methods**' tab, as shown below.

Google

Webmaster Tools

Verify your ownership of **http://www.ihubbusiness.co.uk/**. Learn more.

Recommended method   Alternate methods

○ **HTML tag**
Add a meta tag to your site's home page.

○ **Google Analytics**
Use your Google Analytics account.

○ **Domain name provider**
Sign in to your domain name provider.

[VERIFY]   Not now

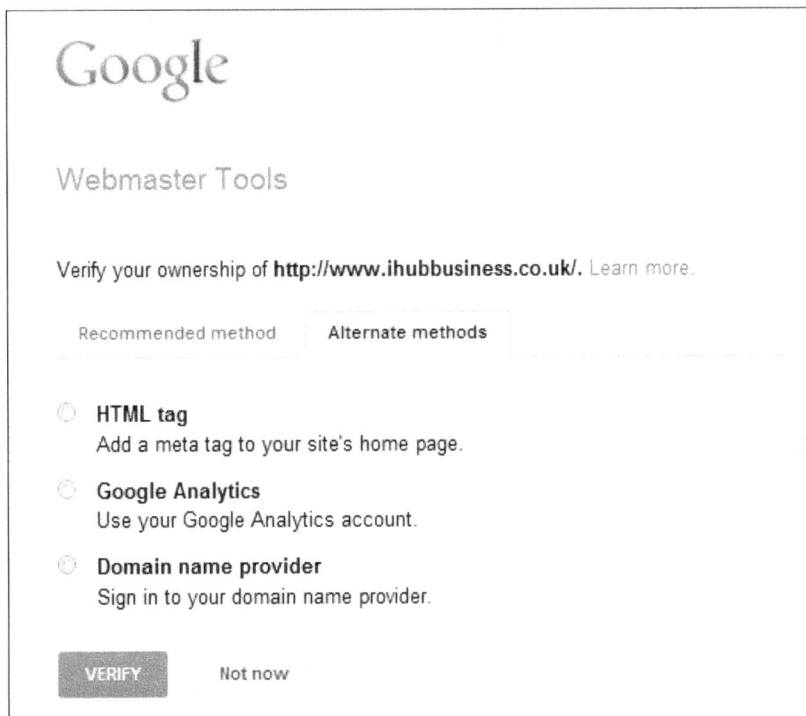

1. You are presented with three options in the Alternate Methods view, as shown in the screenshot above. If, like me, you choose the HTML tag option, you will be presented with a code which you then need to copy and paste into your website HTML. This is not as intimidating as it may sound. All you do here is copy and paste into your website the code given. If you have a WordPress site, go to your dashboard and navigate as follows: go to '**Appearance > Editor > Edit themes**'; locate the following header code : <head>. The code you are given should be then pasted in this section, before the first <body> section. Here is a link to a very clear video that gives you step by step explanation on how to do this: **www.expand2web.com/blog/verify-wordpress-website-google-webmaster-tools**

2. If you are still unsure of how to do this, again you will need to ask your web developer for assistance.

3. Click '**Update file**'.

4. Go back to the Google webmaster tool, and click the **'Verify'** button. Your site should be verified. Now is the time to submit the sitemap you created.

5. Go to the Homepage, find your site and click on its link.

6. Next, locate the **'Submit a sitemap'** button. Type your sitemap.xml inside the box. It is important to include the exact location of the sitemap, so if you stored it in your WordPress subfolder, you would enter in /Word Press/sitemap.xml. Then, click **'Submit sitemap'**.

Do not be alarmed if you are presented with 'Pending' – it may take time.

Optimising for local search and ranking high in your local market

How does local search work though? Well, local search is based on several different methodologies, including the science known as geolocation. Simply put, this is the means of working out where a computer physically is, geographically speaking. It goes a little like this: computer 11.22.33.44 puts out a request to servers for information on Malaysian restaurants. How does the search engine figure out whether the computer is in Manchester or Kuala Lumpur?

To answer this question requires a little knowledge about how search engines work:

1. **Search engines are very literal operators.** If, for example, you typed in "Malaysian restaurants in London", the search engine will display options for Malaysian restaurants – in London, and regardless of where you happen to be.

2. **Search services can also predict your location.** If you are searching via **www.google.co.uk**, it is a good bet that you are in the UK and not in France, for example.

3. **Search engines can look for Internet Protocol (IP) numbers.** These numbers exist to identify computers on the internet. If you have a computer that is connected to the internet, you will have your own unique IP number or IP address as it is sometimes known.

Why employ local search?

There are at least three reasons why you should be interested in local search:

1. People often target their searches by geography, e.g. 'London chiropodist'.

2. Search engines are providing great local search services in order to encourage local searching.

3. Local search services will simply guess where searchers are.

The main search engines have two indexes that provide local data when you do a search. First there are the regular organic search results. The second, local results, provide data from an entirely different place. You may, for example, not be doing too well in the organic results, but you could be doing well in the local results; the site will appear high on the page next to the map provided as shown below.

These are completely different indexes, so different things need to be done for you to rank well in each one.

Example:

If you search for *Pasta York*, Google provides two types of search results:

- Local search results for *Pasta in York*
- Organic search results for *Pasta York*

If however, you are in York and search for 'pasta' – i.e. just the product term pasta without the local term York, Google returns:

- Local search results for pasta in York
- Organic search results for pasta

Ergo, if the searcher uses a local keyword, Google does both a local search and a search of the organic directory for pages that include a local keyword. If the local keyword is not used, Google still does a local search using the local search directory based on where it thinks you are, but as far as the organic search is concerned, Google just looks for the keyword that is put in, and will not modify the search based on where you are.

How to localise your web pages

- Include your full address in your web pages. That is, your street, your city and post code. Ideally, put your address near the top of the page somewhere, as it is better SEO-wise there, than at the footer.

- Include in all your pages the names of all the places you are interested in from a business point of view. So, you can include a list of cities you serve in the footer or sidebar, ideally with links to pages with information about each of these places.

- Create a Contact Us page for every single location you have. Also, put keywords in your Contact Us pages.

- Include your city name in your <TITLE> and Meta Description tags.

- Include city names in link text when linking from other sites to yours, and request others who link to you do the same.

- Mention your city and postcode in the body of your content. You should also place them in header tags, using bold font on some of the references too.

Registering your site for local search

Here are the top three local search engines:

1. Google Maps/Places (www.google.com/local/add)

It is free to use, and offers the ability to add video and imagery. To the user, the service appears to be called Google Maps. However, for businesses the brand Google Places is used.

2. Yahoo! Local (listings.local.yahoo.com)

The interface for Yahoo! local is shown below. It is free or $9.95 per month for an enhanced listing at the time of writing. That's to say, if you want to add imagery, a tagline and a business description.

3. Bing Local Search (www.bing.com/businessportal)

Bing is free, including photographs.

When listing your business, add as much information as possible. Add text with keywords, and as many product and brand names, photos and videos as you can. Google allows you to include video, but you need to first upload it to YouTube, then embed it into your listing. You will need to verify your listing, usually by phone. Google also allows you to post 'live' to your business listing; for example, special promotions or anything of value to customers. You can also request that they send someone to your office to take photos (**www.maps.google.com/help/maps/businessphotos**).

Remember local directories that do not feed data to the major search engines but are still important in their own right. For example, if you owned a sushi bar in St Johns Wood, you should aim to get a review of this into a local directory, such as **www.qype.co.uk**. Other local UK directories include **www.Thomsonlocal.com**, **www.freeindex.co.uk**, **www.thebestof.co.uk**, and **www.yell.com**. A listing with Yellow Pages Yell will get your basic business contact details listed for free.

Ask happy customers to post reviews – this is a tip from my local Chinese health clinic in London, who have attributed almost all of their new business to positive reviews – in return for a small incentive, if necessary. Reviews are useful for two reasons:

1. The number of reviews, or your review star-rating, is thought to have some effect on your ranking in search engines local results.

2. When a customer has to choose which site to click on, they will usually opt for the one with positive reviews.

Good sites to be reviewed at include **www.mumsnet.com**, **www.qype.co.uk**, **www.which.co.uk**, and **www.welovelocal.com**.

SEO expert interview: Red Evolution

David Robinson

David runs Scottish web and search experts Red Evolution. Previously, he worked with other communications agencies in Scotland, and before that, he was part of the web based e-learning department at the University of Aberdeen.

David, how does your company help small businesses with SEO?

Firstly, by using plain English to communicate how to ensure a website attracts the right kind of visitors. I think it's important that any business owner understands, in broad terms, the fundamentals of search engine optimisation.

We then offer them impartial advice, even if that means not securing their business, including help to understand where they currently sit and why, and the work we believe is required to take things forward. This approach usually weeds out those looking for quick fixes, which is good for us; clients like that are impossible to satisfy.

Small businesses tend to avoid investing in SEO because it usually comes with a high price tag. What are your comments on this?

If their business plan suggests the web is an important business acquisition tool they have two choices. They can change their business plan or they can build a website that's going to attract visitors likely to buy from them. It's that simple.

With respect to SEO, they can buy in the expertise they need – and SEO comes with a price tag similar to many other professional services – or they can invest in staff training and carry out the work in-house. The in-house approach can be attractive, but often for all the wrong reasons.

What are the keys to success with 'organic search'?

In my opinion you can invest time and energy looking for a silver bullet – to date there isn't one I'm aware of – or you can create a website that deserves to rank. It's this concept that businesses of all sizes struggle with.

Many are comfortable with what Seth Godin calls the TV Industrial Complex. In this, model businesses that need exposure simply buy it by using interruption marketing. Natural (organic) search or permission marketing turns this on it's head. Of course, PPC [paid search] muddies these waters.

In practical terms, how can an internet 'newbie' get started?

There are some great standard texts available and I would advise reading one of these. A book such as *The Art of SEO* provides a solid foundation.

Of course, there's lots of great and reliable information online, but to a newbie, differentiating the good from the bad, from the plain wrong is a challenge. I would almost always advise sourcing a highly regarded book as the starting point.

Taking this approach, and being realistic, ensures people avoid setting themselves up for a fall.

What advice would you give to someone wishing to use an SEO company?

As with procuring any professional service, it's all about building a relationship. Our best clients are people who've taken the time to get to know us.

In essence, the basic rules of business apply. If someone is making you an offer that seems to good to be true, it almost certainly will be. Do some background work, such as reading a good book, and really engage with two or three potential partners. It's also worth speaking to the agencies' current clients, and from there trust your intuition.

What's new, interesting and cutting edge in SEO right now?

There are some great tools around for managing SEO campaigns, tools that are easy to use and help you get to the important stuff quickly. That said, Google is still trying to deliver the most relevant results to users, just like it always has, so creating what users want remains our priority.

Finally, what one piece of advice would you offer someone who is looking to get their site onto the front page of Google, etc?

From a natural or organic search perspective, don't look for quick fixes. From a pay per click point of view, hire a professional to set up your campaign.

How to get your products listed in product directories

Did you know that most product search results do not come from the major search engines' organic search indexes? Most product related searches are being made outside the major search engines. The major search engines have their own product indexes. Google, which already has its PPC index, organic search index and local search index, also has a product search index called Google Product

Search. Yahoo! has its Yahoo! shopping index provided by **PriceGrabber.com**, while Bing has Bing Shopping.

Imagine the scenario: you have worked very hard to get your site into the organic search index and you rank well when people search for your products. However, most of the search results being presented to your prospective clients do not come from organic search indexes; rather, they come from Amazon's index or eBay's or even one of the major search engine's product search indexes.

If you sell products, you really have to list them within product indexes. Most of these directories will require payment, though not all of them do. Google's Product Search, for example, is completely free. The ones that do expect you to pay, only charge when someone clicks a link to visit your site, or even when a sale is made, so even these directories may be worth a punt.

There are three types of product indexes:

1. **Single product indexes**: You simply list your products in the index. When your products pop up, it is hoped that the searcher will click through to your site.

2. **Ecommerce sites**: With these you are effectively putting your products into someone else's shop. It may not be obvious to your buyers that they are buying from a third party either.

3. **Classified-ad sites**: With these, adverts about your products are periodically posted, with links back to your site. There are quite a few of these sites, but they pale in significance next to Craigslist.

Product indexes

Google Product (www.google.com/merchants): Google's product search is a useful way to expose your products to more shoppers on one of the most popular search engines on the web.

Your products will appear in the Product Search engine, and may also appear on Google's standard search results, depending on the relevance of the product to the search being performed. Google has created a service that helps online retailers list and submit products to Google's Product Search, Product Ads, and Commerce Search offerings. This service, called Google Merchant Center, can accept a data feed of product information (**google.com/merchants**). For detailed information on how to go about listing your products in Google, please read this excellent article by Practical Commerce (**www.practicale-commerce.com/articles/3239-Formatting-a-Product-Spreadsheet-for-Google -Merchant-Center**). Preparing and updating your product data feed can be time consuming, but this article can help you.

Other search engines to list products:

- Yahoo! Shopping (**www.uk.shopping.yahoo.com**)
- Price Grabber (**www.pricegrabber.co.uk**)
- Bing Shopping (**advertising.microsoft.com/small-business/search-advertising/bing-shopping**)

- Ask.com & Pronto (**merchant.pronto.com**)
- BizRate & Shopzilla (**www.shopzilla.co.uk**)
- The Find (**www.thefind.com**)
- NexTag (**www.nextag.com**)
- Shopping.com/DealTime.com/Epinions.com (**uk.shopping.com**)
- PriceSCAN (**www.pricescan.com**)
- Shopwiki (**www.shopwiki.com**)

Most of these systems will expect you to pay. There are three types of systems to look out for:

1. **Free**: You have no direct control over your position; however you do not have to pay for any traffic that you get from the site. Google Product Search, Shopmania and TheFind are all free for basic listings.

2. **Cost per click**: You do not have any control over your positioning again, because there is no bidding and you pay a fixed fee per click. An example is Yahoo! Shopping.

3. **Cost per click with bidding**: Here you bid on the position you want. Those who bid the most get front page listing.

Ecommerce sites

These are the indexes which are maintained by ecommerce or merchant sites, which will allow third parties to sell products through their stores. The two most important ones are Amazon (**www.amazon.co.uk**) and eBay (**www.ebay.co.uk**).

With the auction sites, you simply sell your products as at an auction and handle the transactions yourself. With the retail sites, your product is placed into a directory and if anyone purchases your product, the retail site will handle the transaction process, sending you the information so that you can ship the product. You will later be sent the money, minus any commission.

Why should you do this when you have a store on your own website?

Most people who are looking for the products you stock may not find your site directly; they will go through product sites such as Amazon and eBay. Amazon gets around 280 million searches a month, and some of these are for products that you will market. You will be left out of this huge pie unless you join them. eBay is one of the top three ecommerce sites in the world and it gets around 650 million searches a month – more than twice Amazon's number. It is not just an auction site; it also hosts thousands of stores, many of which sell fixed-price goods in addition to taking part in the auction. It is worth spending time looking through both of these sites, as they each have their own way of 'doing business' with merchants such as yourself.

There are also tools that can help you with the process. Single Feed (**singlefeed.com**) will feed data about your products such as name, stock levels, price, and other attributes, on your behalf, to up to seventeen different systems, including Google Product Search and Bing, for a small monthly fee. Your competition will probably be using these systems – so why don't you?

Classified ad sites

Craigslist (**www.craigslist.co.uk**) receives over 20 billion page views a month. You post your products in the listings, with links back to your site. These links are no-follow*,however, so while they will not help you from a search engine standpoint, they get so much traffic to them it would be silly to ignore them. Indeed, many businesses promote their products and services very successfully through classified-ad sites; in particular Craigslist and **www.backpage.com**.

*No-follow links are links that are ignored, or not 'crawled' by the search engine spiders we discussed earlier. This means that the links will make no difference to your search engine rankings.

Quick summary

- Make your site visible by using keywords and getting your title tags and meta descriptions right.

- Organic search – i.e. traffic that comes through the search engines, is the most cost-effective way to get people to your site.

- Work to get links to point to your site using all the tips discussed in this chapter.

- Make sure your products are listed in the relevant directories, and don't forget the importance of local search.

Chapter 5

Paid Search – Introducing Pay Per Click (PPC), Step By Step

In this chapter you will learn how to set up a robust Google Advertising campaign from start to testing, incorporating these important essentials:

- Understanding the difference between paid and organic searches.
- Setting up an AdWords campaign – step by step.
- Creating Ads and Groups – tips and techniques.
- The role of landing pages.
- Running and monitoring your AdWords campaign.
- Competitor analysis.

Print advertising – for so long the mainstay of marketing for small and large businesses – has suffered from a significant decline in popularity, due in large part to its limitations. For example, how do you ensure that only those who have expressed an interest in your business or product will see your advert? Furthermore, with print advertising, you pay up front, whether or not your advertising campaign has been successful. In contrast, online advertising – of which pay per click is the most common form – ensures that your advert appears only when an internet searcher types in a word or phrase that is relevant to your product or service. This means that the right people are more likely to see your advert. In addition, you can amend your advert however much you wish, and best of all; you only pay when the user clicks on your advertisment. If you get no clicks you do not need to pay.

Paid search vs. Organic search: what is the difference?

Table A – Paid Search

Paid search (pay per click) advantages	Paid search disadvantages
Immediate visibility – your advert will appear on the first page of search results, depending on the keyword.	Paid search is not regarded as favourably as organic search – you've paid for it
Cost effective – your campaign can be turned on and off according to your needs	Can be expensive in the long term. As your competition bid on your keywords, your costs can rise – this could be a problem if this is your main means of getting the visibility you need.
You are in control – write or change your adverts when and how you wish. Your copy appears as you write it.	It is time consuming to manage and track.
Design costs are low – no graphic design team is needed, as it's just the words you are paying for.	There is an art to writing great advertisements – a badly written advert is an expensive advert.
Space restriction on copy encourages you to get to your core benefits quickly.	

Table B – Organic Search

Organic search – advantages	Organic search – disadvantages
Seen as more credible. Searchers have more faith in organic search listings than sponsored listings (PPC).	The process can be difficult to understand, especially for small businesses.
The results are longer lasting, giving you a consistent presence – it takes time to lose your rank.	It does take a while to achieve a good rank – anything from three months upwards.
Generally a good return on investment.	It is subject to the whims of Google's algorithms.

How to set up an AdWords campaign

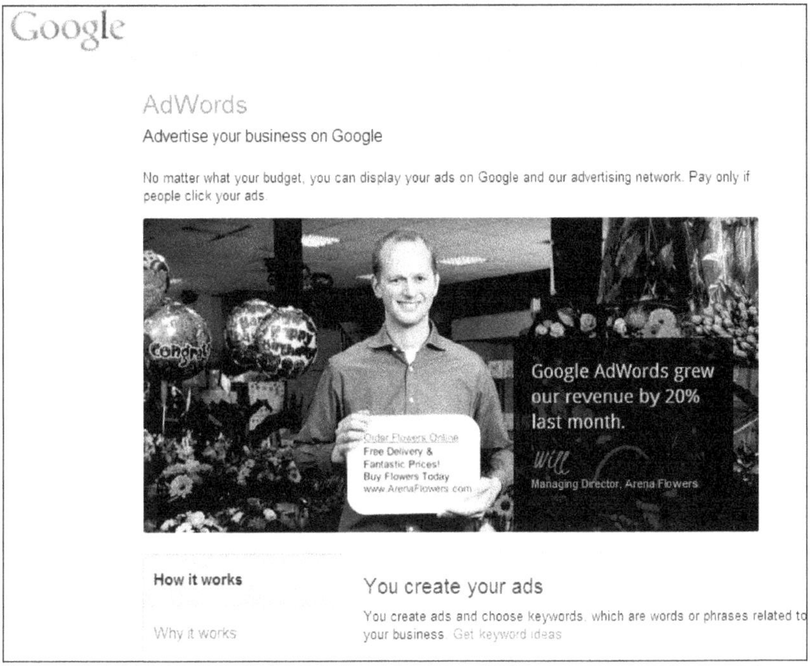

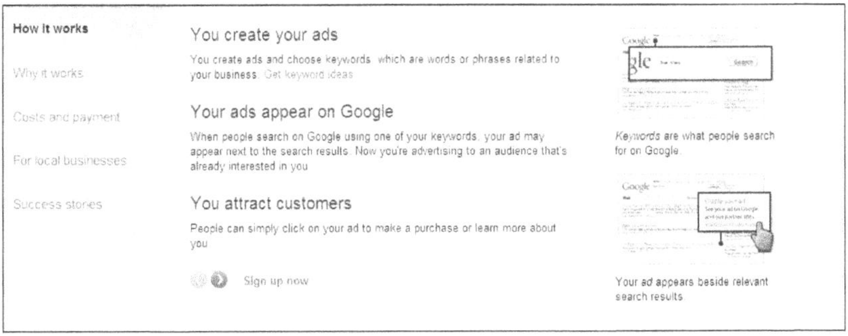

Step 1: The first thing you need to do is set up your AdWords account

- You need to go to **www.adwords.google.com** and click on the '**Sign up now**' link. You will be taken to a web page that will look like the one below:

- You will need to follow the instructions given to create your Google AdWords account.

- Set your time zone and currency preferences. Click '**Continue**' and Google will let you know that it has sent a verification email to your email account. Once this arrives, simply click the link and you will be taken into AdWords.

- Even if you are new to AdWords, scroll down until you find the '**For experienced advertisers**' section, and click the '**Start creating advanced campaigns**' link. I am sure this is deliberately worded so as to intimidate! Clicking on this link will avoid you devolving all your choices to Google, who may spend more of your budget than necessary. It will take you to the following (or similar) page:

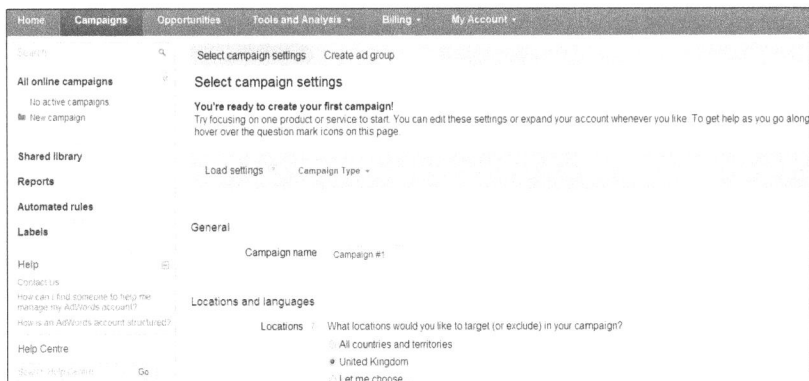

Step 2: Select your search options

- When planning your campaign, you will be presented with a choice of search engines, and also devices, that your adverts will appear on. The basic choices are Google Search, Search Partners and the Content Network.

- Google will recommend you to have your adverts shown across 'All available sites and devices'. In my opinion, it is best to ignore this and instead set your campaign to Google Search only: each of the three options needs to be treated differently for you to be truly effective.

- I suggest you begin with Google Search and get your campaign up and running profitably, before adding Search Partners into the mix. Then, and only then, set up a separate campaign for the Content Network. That is, only if you really need to.

- Google will also allow you to choose whether to target mobile devices as well as standard computers. Again, I suggest sticking with computers at first, unless mobile is key to your marketing strategy.

Step 3: Manage your advert rotation

- Once your Ad Group has been created – and I will be covering this later on – you can decide how Google rotates your adverts.

- It is best practice to have more than one advertisement, so I suggest you do so.

- Rotation simply involves Google cycling through all of your adverts, instead of simply showing the same advert every time someone's search matches your keywords.

- Google will, by default, give preference to advertisements with higher click-through rates, so the adverts that outperform will be shown more often. The problem with this is that it does not help you determine which adverts work best. You will have little information about all of your advertisements if this is the case. Therefore, instruct Google to show your adverts in strict rotation.

Step 4: Manage your campaign settings

- Go to your AdWords account and click **'Create your first campaign'**.

- On the Campaign Settings screen, give your campaign a name. Underneath, find **'Locations'** and select the narrowest range of locations that will ensure the most interested people will see your advertisement.

- Under **'Networks, devices and extensions'** click **'Let me choose'** and deselect all the given options except for Google Search. Deselect Mobile Devices unless this is an important market for you. The fewer the variables in your campaign, the easier it will be to tweak here and there.

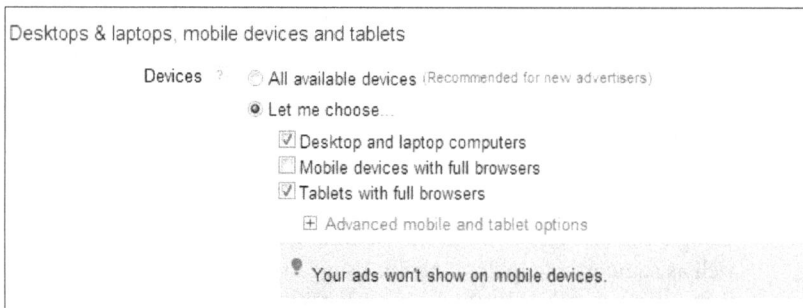

Desktops & laptops, mobile devices and tablets

Devices   ?   ○ All available devices (Recommended for new advertisers)
                 ◉ Let me choose...
                    ☑ Desktop and laptop computers
                    ☐ Mobile devices with full browsers
                    ☑ Tablets with full browsers
                       ⊞ Advanced mobile and tablet options

                    💡 Your ads won't show on mobile devices.

- Under **'Bidding and Budget'** select **'I'll manually set my bids for clicks'** so you can decide how much each click is worth to you, rather than having Google tell you. The idea is to pay as little as possible, to achieve a good position in the sponsored listings, and you will only be able to do this if you manually set your bidding prices and note where this positions you. Now, set your budget. Google spreads it over a month so that on any given day your actual costs may exceed the daily limit set here, but not by a huge amount. I suggest setting your budget anywhere between £3 and £10 as a small business. It is very important to watch your spend carefully as, if a lot of users click on your advertisment, your bill can rise significantly. If in doubt, err on the lower side.

- Click **'Save and continue'**, and Google will ask you to create your first advertisement. A good suggestion is to put in dummy text here until you set up your Ad Groups – which I cover in the next section. Type your main keyword into the keyword box. Set a cost per click by clicking **'Estimate search traffic'**, and then pick a value below the lowest estimate. Again, always go low at this stage. Google will then take you through to the billing process to pay.

- Once you have settled your bill, Google will automatically turn on your campaign. You will not yet be ready to start spending money so click the **'Campaigns'** tab, click **'Enabled'** and select **'Pause'**. This means your campaign is ready, but inactive.

Creating adverts and Ad Groups
What is an Ad Group?

Ad Groups are, quite literally, groups of adverts. You would typically have at least two Ad Groups, if not more, ideally. Ad Groups allows you to build clusters of keywords and test multiple versions of the advert you create for each group, which then allows you to carry out an analysis of which keywords and messages give you the most profitable click-through rate and, ultimately, the most profitable conversion rates. What you do is create an ad group out of each of your main keywords. For example, if you were a party supplies business then you might decide that two of your keyword groups could be 'party bags for boys' and 'personalised party bags'. Putting each of these into its own ad group means you can write adverts aimed specifically at people who are looking for party bags for boys, and separate adverts for those looking for personalised party supplies. You can also point each advertisement at its own landing page (we will look at landing pages later on in this chapter), which will increase your conversion rate and relevance.

Before you begin creating your Ad Groups, you will need to understand how the bidding process works. In general, the higher up Google's sponsored rankings your advertisement appears, the more clicks you should get. However, the catch is that you will need to bid more for these positions, which will squeeze your budget. The important thing we are after is for you to attract the most profitable traffic to your site for the lowest cost.

How does the bidding process work?

When a search term is typed into Google, it holds an 'auction' amongst potential advertisers and then determines where each advert will appear. Google gives each advert a 'Quality Score' out of ten, and then calculates its 'Ad Rank' by multiplying the Quality Score by the maximum bid. The Quality Score (QS) is based on three things: the advertisment's historical click-through rate, the relevance of the advert, and the landing page to which it directs the user. The most important of these factors is the click-through rate, which to Google equates to a 'vote' by searchers; it accounts for around 60% of the QS, followed by relevance at around 30% and then your landing page at around 10%.

Example

Imagine there are two advertisers. The first has set a maximum cost per click of £2 and the other £1. If they both have the same QS, the first advertiser will appear above the second, simply because he has bid more. However if the first advertiser has a QS of 2 and an Ad Rank of 4 (£2 multiplied by 2) and the second has a QS of 6, the second will appear above the first because they have an Ad Rank of 6 (£1 mutlipied by 6). This is why one advertising competitor can appear above another, even if he or she has bid less.

Tips for writing adverts

The following tips have been inspired by AdWords guru, Perry Mason:

Tip 1: Use punctuation marks from your computer's keyboard.

- Mason suggests applying various "filters" to your adverts. Each filter forces you to write the advert a different way than you might ordinarily do. Here are some examples of filters: # – $, % & ' ' " " / ~ : ; ( ) So, for example, if you chose to use dashes or quotes in your advertisement, you will likely find yourself writing a different advert than you may have done if you did not use dashes or quotes. Here's an example of an advert written around dashes:

  Popular Internet Term, Complex Words – Easy Definitions, Immediate download – Free PDF Jargon Buster. www.easydoesit.co.uk

Tip 2: Write adverts that nod to any of our five senses.

E.g. *Deep Tissue Massage. Relieve tense and aching muscles. Feel your stiff joints and muscles loosen – book now.* www.experttouchmassage.com

Tip 3: Reference the well-known – with permission.

E.g. *Exquisite ruby pendants. Transform any outfit now. (Similar worn by Kiera Knightly & Emma Watson.)* www.thissiterocks.com

Note the use of brackets in this ad, too.

Tip 4: Use Metaphors.

E.g. *Will Your Event Be A Circus of Utter Chaos, Or the Proudest Moment of Your Career?* **www.TheLondonEvent.com**

Tip 5: Use Incentives.

E.g. *Trial offers, very long guarantees, free samples, etc.*

Tip 6: Create a sense of urgency.

E.g. *Deadline is midnight August 22.*

(According to Mason, deadline dates are rarely seen in Google ads, but can be highly effective.)

Creating your adverts

If you have followed steps1-4 above, about how to set up an AdWords campaign, you will have created a campaign with a dummy ad, which you paused. Now follow these instructions:

- Go to your AdWords campaign and click the **'Ads'** tab. There, you will find your existing dummy advert. Click on the **'Keywords'** tab; add in your keywords – one per line. Click the pencil icon to edit the headline, body text, display URL (the first one) and destination URL. The display URL is the address seen on your advertisement; the destination URL is the one users are taken to if they click. For example, a landing page URL can be displayed as your domain URL. Your advert will only be allowed if your display URL points to the same domain as the destination URL.

- After you click the **'Save'** button, you can then create your second advertisement by selecting **'Text ad'** for your Ad Group from the options in the **'New Ad'** drop-down menu. Create your new advert using the editor. Make sure you use different text so that you get a clear result when you split-test your two adverts. You could, for example, change the headline and body copy of the advert, but leave the display URL and the landing page the same. Or, you could switch round the headline with one of the description lines. The idea is to be clear on which combination of wording gets the best results.

Tip

Visit AdWords guru Perry Mason's blog (**www.perrymason.com**) for more useful information about creating adverts and advertising.

In the example below – and you will not see it all – I created three ad groups, with two adverts in each group, making a total of six adverts. The groups are Internet Marketing Strategies, Internet Marketing Small Business and Internet Marketing Solutions. Two of the groups point to my home page, while the final group points to a landing page (discussed further in the next section). I am testing out two things: the performance of the adverts themselves and the effectiveness of the landing page.

Now, go to your Campaign Settings and hit **'Advanced Settings'**. Click on **'Ad delivery'**, **'Ad rotation'**, **'Frequency capping'**, and pick **'Rotate: Show ads more evenly'**. As you will see in the example below, you will be told that you should leave this set to **'Optimise'**. However, by choosing to have your adverts shown evenly, you are ensuring all variations get enough clicks for you to be able to choose a winner. You can then delete the losing advert and create another variation of the best ad.

Bidding and budget

Bidding option   **Focus on clicks, manual maximum CPC bidding**   Edit

Budget   **£5.00/day**   Edit

Delivery method (advanced)

Ad extensions

Use this option to show relevant business information with your text ads. You can create and manage your extensions from the Ad extensions tab. Take a tour.

Advanced settings

Schedule: Start date, end date, ad scheduling
Ad delivery: Ad rotation, frequency capping

Ad rotation   **Rotate evenly: Show ads more evenly for 90 days, then optimise for clicks**   Edit

Frequency capping   **No cap on impressions**
Display Network only   Your campaign must be opted in to the Display Network to use this feature.

+ New ad ▾   Change status... ▾   Automate ▾   More actions

   Ad   Ad group   L

Below are the list of ads and adgroups I am running, showing 3 different adgroups with adverts for each

Small Business Marketing
Need Online Marketing Support?
- Free Membership - Sign up Today!
www.ihubbusiness.co.uk

Internet Marketing Small Business

Are You A Small Business?
Small Business Internet Marketing
Learn strategies that work. Free!
www.ihubbusiness.co.uk

Internet Marketing Small Business

Learn Internet Marketing
Does Your Small Business Need A
Push? We Help. You Grow. Free.
www.ihubbusiness.co.uk

Internet Marketing Strategies

Internet Marketing Help
Need Internet Marketing Help?
Learn Strategies That Work. Free!
www.ihubbusiness.co.uk

Internet Marketing Strategies

Small Business Blogging
Get a Free Blog Site Today!
Post articles, upload Images& video

Internet Marketing Solutions

The role of landing pages

An example of **Mailchimp.com**'s landing page:

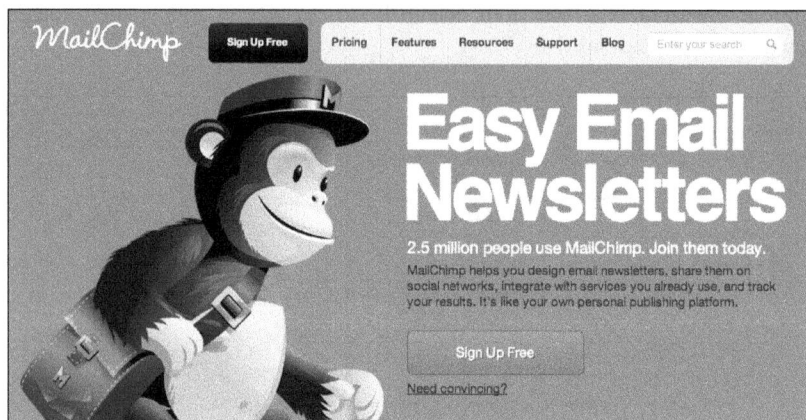

Clicking on an advert is just the first step; Google allows you to track your visitors right through the process. There are two important steps to the process. The first is creating a landing page – the page where your visitors arrive when they click on an advertisment. The second is setting up conversion tracking. If you decide to create a landing page other than your homepage, I suggest you do so now. Landing pages are generally considered best practice for advertising purposes, and much more effective than using your homepage.

These days landing page templates are easily available, and free (although you may need to hand over your email details). A landing page is made up of two parts: a series of benefits and a clear call to action. You need to make it very clear what action you want the user to take – whether that is to buy your product now or sign up to your mailing list. Once you have a template, it may be necessary to ask your web designer to help you put it together. A landing page should ideally have a clear and articulated value so that visitors understand immediately what is on offer. In other words the information on the page should answer two questions: "What is it?" and "Why should I care?" The main title of your landing page should be used as a very clear statement of what you are offering to enable an understanding of the offering of your page.

Landing pages should:

- Contain just one single message, and just one call to action (CTA).

- Use plenty of whitespace, contrast, colour and directional cues, such as arrows.

- Contain a proportionate amount of information requested based on the perceived value of the offering. For example, you do not need to ask for every piece of contact information from your visitors if all you are offering is a newsletter or ebook.

- Use credible testimonials with visuals to encourage a positive response.

Tips

- Whilst there are plenty of companies online that specialise in landing pages, there are a few which are truly outstanding, such as **www.unbounce.com** and **www.clicky.com**.

- For further reading on what makes a great landing page, have a look at this excellent post by Dr Dave Chaffey: **www.smartinsights.com/conversion-optimisation/landing-page-optimisation/perfect-landing-page**.

Running and monitoring your AdWords campaign

Once your campaign is up and running, you will need to set up conversion tracking to monitor the effectiveness of the campaign.

There are seven key metrics for an AdWords campaign: impressions, clicks, click-through rate, cost per click, conversion number, conversion rate and cost per conversion. The first four are always shown in the AdWords' control panel; however, the conversion rate and cost per conversion are not, and these are without a doubt the most important metrics for your business. Without the conversion rate and the cost per conversion, you will have no way of knowing how much you are spending in marketing per sale, and therefore will not be able to evaluate the profitability of your campaign. Below is a screenshot showing the different metrics you can expect to see in your AdWords control panel:

	Ad group	Status	Default Max. CPC	Display Network Max. CPC	+ Clicks	Impr.	CTR	Avg. CPC	Cost	Avg. Pos.	Conv. (1-per-click)	Cost / conv. (1-per-click)	Conv. rate (1-per-click)	View-through Conv.
	Internet Marketing Small Business	Eligible	£1.50	auto	35	2,196	1.59%	£1.19	£41.71	3.4	0	£0.00	0.00%	0
	Internet Marketing Strategies	Eligible	£1.50	auto	18	6,202	0.29%	£1.30	£23.39	4.5	0	£0.00	0.00%	0
	Internet Marketing Solutions	Eligible	£1.50	auto	0	34	0.00%	£0.00	£0.00	6.2	0	£0.00	0.00%	0

There are three main pieces of data you need to understand:

1. **Impressions (Impr)**: Each time your advert is seen, this is called an 'impression'. In the 'Keywords' tab, you can see how many of those impressions were triggered by each keyword. If you sort the list by impressions, you will see which of your keywords generated the most views of your advertisement.

2. **Clicks**: Your clicks are the number of times your advert was actually clicked on. Again, you can view the number of clicks for each keyword under the 'Keywords' tab. Your click-through rate is the percentage of impressions that resulted in a click. Do not get too excited about this figure however; what counts is the amount of sales you receive! That said, when it comes to deciding which advert is performing better than another, you would need to look at the number of clicks and click-through rate.

3. **Conversions**: A 'conversion' is what you want it to be. In other words, it is the action you want the visitor to take when they get to your site; whether that is signing up to an email list or making a purchase. The number of conversions, the conversion rate, and the cost per conversion, are the most important three figures to track. Together they sum up the profitability – or lack of – of your business. The number of conversions will give you an indication of your turnover and the cost per conversion will be the indicator of your cost of doing business. If the number of your conversions drops, or the cost per conversion rises, take action to work out why this is the case. Then resolve the situation; it could be simply factors in the marketplace, a new entrant, or even your shopping cart process. Successful internet businesses will often boast conversion rates in the region of 1-2%, while some will be higher, and some lower. A conversion rate of, say 0.5%, will require 200 visitors per sale. If you have paid for this traffic, then you need to have a product with a pretty high purchase price to make this profitable.

A word of caution. Do make sure you have enough figures to be statistically valid. For example, you should have at least 20 conversions before you draw any conclusions about the effectiveness of your campaign. If you have a conversion rate of 1%, then you will need 2,000 clicks! If we assume a CTR (click-through rate) of 5% you would need 40,000 impressions (2000 ÷ 0.05).

Tips

- To calculate the number of visitors you need per sale, simply divide 100 by the conversion you are seeking, e.g. 100 ÷ 0.5 = 200.

- To calculate how many clicks you need, divide the number of conversions by your conversion rate: 20 ÷ 0.01 = 2000.

Google's free to use Conversion Optimiser will help you to maximise your return on investment by automatically getting you the most possible conversions for your budget. The tool will help you measure how clicks on your adverts lead to desired actions, such as sales or leads. Conversions happen when a click on your advertisement leads directly to a business goal/objective, such as a sign up, a purchase or a download. Conversion tracking will measure events like these on your website.

By tracking your conversions you will have an insight into how effective your advertisements are; conversion tracking will also help you identify which effective advertisements and keywords are the best for your business.

You will need the help of your web developer to take advantage of this free tool; that is someone who can confidently edit your site's HTML code to add some tracking code. What this code will do is place what is called a 'cookie' on a user's computer or mobile phone when they click on your advertisement.

What's a cookie?

A **cookie**, also known as a **browser cookie**, is usually a small piece of data – a text file – sent from a website and stored in a user's web browser while the user is browsing a website. When the user browses the same website in the future, any data stored in the cookie can be retrieved by the website to notify the website of the user's previous activity. They are therefore very useful widgets for the purposes of marketing and data collection.

If the user reaches one of your conversion pages, AdWords looks for the cookie and records this as a conversion for you.

You can learn how to set up and manage the conversion optimiser for your business here: **support.google.com/adwords/answer/2472674**

Competitor analysis

For outstanding competitor intelligence data and keyword research data that will improve the return on your pay per click investment, look no further than **www.keywordspy.com**.

The tool, which allows you to have a lifetime 'free trial' account, gives you information on who your top competitors are by search engine, by their most profitable keywords, by the adverts they are running, by their landing pages and by their ranking position for each keyword. In addition, you can see how much they are bidding for each click on a keyword. To obtain this information manually would be nigh on impossible, so this really is a great asset to your internet marketing toolkit. There are some great YouTube videos that take you through using Keyword Spy, such as the 'Keyword Spy Intelligent Keyword Tracking' video which is worth tracking down on YouTube, as well as tutorial videos from the company itself (**support.keywordspy.com/videos**).

YouTube:

www.youtube.com/watch?v=3uM4aUjmtdQ
www.youtube.com/watch?v=e3dVEJ2zcyg

Quick summary

- Pay per click is a great way to drive targeted traffic to your site.

- When planning a campaign, make sure you take ownership of every step – do not leave this to Google. Track your conversions and respond accordingly.

Chapter 6

Permission Based Internet Marketing

In this chapter you will learn:

- What customer relationship management is and how cross-sell and up-sell can be used to boost your sales.
- What permission based internet marketing is and its relevance today.
- How to succeed with email marketing.
- Credibility factors that encourage people to buy.

A business that does not build customer relationships will only succeed if every transaction is profitable. The costs of running your business, including the costs of production, must add up to less than the revenue received from customers. Online, this is becoming increasingly hard to achieve due to the rising cost of online advertising.

Successful businesses, such as Boots and Tesco, understand that fundamentally, long-term relationships need to be built with customers to encourage them to continue to shop there. Boots has its Advantage card, Tesco has its Clubcard and Sainsbury's has its Nectar card. In this chapter you will see the tremendous capability you have to get closer to customers, to understand them better and target relevant communications; in short, you will learn how to build relationships with your customers. Email marketing is one of the most effective forms of online marketing, and also one of the most popular as a means of acquiring and retaining your customers.

Customer relationship management and how cross-sell and up-sell can be used to boost your sales

The challenge that faces businesses both large and small is that the internet suffers from a lack of trust, despite it being the first destination for online searches. It is this that contributes to the low conversion rates of so many websites – you are doing well if you achieve a 2% conversion. This means that more than 98 out of every 100 visitors who have come to your site by clicking on an advert do not buy. This itself is a generous estimation – many businesses fail because they cannot make their PPC 'pay'. Part of the problem is that customers and potential customers are exposed to limitless interruptions each day and now condition themselves to 'switch off' or 'tune out' at will.

Customer Relationship Management (CRM), which is also referred to as Customer Development or Customer Management, is an established marketing approach to building and sustaining long-term business with customers. There are four elements to customer relationship management:

1. Customer selection – define your target customers.

2. Customer acquisition – define the actions you need to take to form relationships with them.

3. Customer retention – define the actions you need to take to keep them.

4. Customer extension – define how you can get more from your customers; i.e. more customers or customers spending more.

Relationships and retention are the key elements of an effective CRM model. In their renowned cross-industry study, Reichheld and Sasser (1990, Harvard Business Review, September – October, pp.105-11) estimated that by reducing customer defections by just 5%, profitability could be increased by 25% to 85%.

Seven best practice activities for a healthy CRM model

1. Using your website to gain more customers, from generating leads, through conversion, to an online or offline sale using email and web based information to encourage purchase and repeat buying.

2. Getting a high coverage of email addresses (< 95% of your customer base) and integrating customer profile information from other databases to enable targeting.

3. Providing online personalisation – online features which can automatically recommend the 'next-best product'.

4. Providing online customer service facilities – such as Frequently Asked Questions (FAQs).

5. Ensuring that first time buyers have a great customer experience, which encourages them to buy again.

6. Going for a multi-channel approach to reach your customers, as they use different media as part of the buying process and customer lifecycle.

7. Applying permission and email marketing to support cross-sell and up-sell, this is discussed below.

The cross-sell and up-sell

Businesses can make money in three main ways. Firstly, by gaining new business or new customers – this however is the hardest and most expensive way. The second way is to encourage existing customers to return to their website to buy from them again. The third and final way – and this is where cross-sell and up-sell comes in – is to increase the transaction value of each order.

How you can use the cross-sell and up-sell

The cross-sell and up-sell need to be triggered when a customer adds something to their shopping basket. If you were selling iPads then your customers may need an iPad case. Therefore, when your customer adds an iPad to their basket, it's a great idea to say to them, "Do you want an iPad case to go with your iPad?" This is known as the cross-sell. At the same time, if someone is buying a £400 iPad from you, how do you know that they wouldn't buy a £600 iPad from you with bells and whistles on it if they understood the benefits of the additional features? Imagine if they added the £400 iPad to their shopping basket and they were presented with the option to buy a better value iPad, with a large number of clear additional features and benefits, e.g. "You may prefer our iPad 999 which can programme your mind to help you do more, live longer, and feel better." I think you get the idea. This is called 'up-selling'. Clicking on an invitation link to purchase the more expensive iPad will replace the iPad originally selected with the more expensive one. Shopping cart systems you may want to consider that accommodate this cross-sell/up-sell feature include **www.1shoppingcart.com/features/3** and **www.myizzonet.com**, which both offer a free trial period. Christina Hill's blog has plenty of tips on using shopping carts: **shoppingcartqueen.com/blog**

Ideas for accommodating cross-selling and up-selling in your marketing

Think about complementary products. If you are selling golf clubs, for example, you can also offer a bag, balls, lessons and accessories. To gain the extra sale, you might simply have to mention that the other products or services are available.

Post expert recommendations. One way to facilitate cross-selling and up-selling success is to cite endorsements or recommendations from professionals, gurus or experts in your niche. This could be a chef's recommendation on a menu, or lists of related items that other customers have purchased on a website. A great example of this is when you buy a book from **Amazon.com**. Amazon automatically lists other books purchased by people who bought the same book you just ordered.

Timing is everything. Cross-selling and up-selling can occur at different times, depending on the products and services you are selling. In some cases, the best time is while a customer is trying something out. If they are looking at your low priced section of goods, for example, but do not place anything in their shopping basket, it could be that they might need a higher priced model. You could invite them to view some of your higher priced models if they had not found what they were looking for. In a similar vein, if you are a fashion retailer and a customer is browsing your trousers section you could suggest browsing your range of belts to go with the trousers. Once a buying decision has been made by a customer on your site, you could consider adding other items – such as an extended warranty.

Offer a range of prices. If you suggest three items to complement a product, consider offering a mix of price points. Your customers are more likely to go for the cheapest items as impulse buying kicks in.

Consider offering product or service bundles. Bundling is a popular and effective way to entice customers to purchase an entire group of items that go together. Offering a price break on package deals should also help you to close the sale.

Permission marketing and its relevance today

Permission marketing was coined by the renowned marketer Seth Godin, (**www.sethgodin.typepad.com**) author of *Permission Marketing: Turning Strangers into Friends and Friends into Customers*. Permission marketing is best characterised using just three words: "anticipated, relevant and personal" (Godin, 1999).

Broadly, it works thus:

Customers are attracted to your site, for example, by pay per click advertising, links on social media or recommendation. They are then invited to 'opt-in' ('buy' in) to a mutually beneficial, long-term relationship with you, with the inducement of an incentive. Opting in to emails is law in most, if not all, countries now. Ideally, you should identify each customer on their first website visit and subsequent visits. Common methods of identification are use of cookies or asking a customer to register. In subsequent customer contacts, additional information can be obtained.

Using the privilege given to you by the customer to market to them offers a programme of added value content over time; for example, you can continually offer the customer more education about your product or service.

Reinforce the incentive/s to continue to maintain this permission. Offer opt-out avenues – in other words, the option not to continue to be contacted by you in the same way – but you can minimise the likelihood of this happening by giving your potential clients a longer route to remove themselves from your website. For example, instead of offering an opt-out from all services, you could take those wishing to opt-out to a landing page. This landing page provides a complete list of services or products you offer and then asks the individual to select which services/products or types of messages they wish to no longer receive. The result is that you maintain the permission to email to this individual when promoting the specific products, services, or communication types they've identified.

If you are not yet in the position of having multiple products or services, a similar example can still be effective. When taking individuals who wish to opt out to a landing page, show them the type of information they'll be missing out on if they chose to opt out. For example, you could point to offers that will only be valid to opted-in recipients. Promise of access to these features will help to minimise opt-out rates.

The most productive way to minimise your opt-out rate is to offer something of value to your customers so that they want to stay. Whether it's the promise of valuable information that they could receive in the future, or a premium that serves as an incentive, it is important to focus on growing your customer lists, whilst at the same time minimizing opt-out rates.

Over time, leverage the permission your customers give you towards a profitable outcome. A good rule of thumb is to provide mostly information that educates, with only a small proportion of the email leading the customer to a purchase. Another tip is to send one sales orientated message out of every five messages.

Principles of permission marketing

Here are marketing expert Dr Dave Chaffey's principles of permission marketing, which show how Seth Godin's principals can be applied to digital environments:

- Consider selective opt-in communications – i.e. what do you want your visitors to opt-in to? Options for you to consider include:
    - Content – news, products, offers, events.
    - Frequency – weekly, monthly, or quarterly alerts.
    - Channel – email, direct mail, phone or SMS. Format text vs. HTML.
- Create a 'common customer profile' – Chaffey recommends three levels of data:
    - Level 1 – Contact details and key profile fields only.
    - Level 2 – Includes preferences.
    - Level 3 – Includes full purchase and response behaviour.
- Offer a range of opt-in incentives, for example you could offer a gift, or the chance to save money or win a prize.
- The point is that you should not make opt-out too easy – instead of 'unsubscribe', you can offer a link to a web form to update a profile, which includes the option to unsubscribe.

- Monitor click-throughs to different types of content, monitor engagement of individual customers with email communications, and send a reminder to those who don't open the email first time. A good example is the company Boden. Those who have not bought items over a period – whether online or offline through their catalogue – are sent a personalised letter and/or email with a significant voucher discount to tempt them back online.

- Create an outbound contact strategy. How many communications will you send per month? How many offers will you give out? How will you link your offline with your online efforts?

Using auto responders in your permission based marketing

Auto responders are a great way of using automation in marketing. It takes on average seven messages or so before a prospect makes a purchase. An autoresponder will make it easier for you to reach out to your customers by sending out communications to them on your behalf, through an automated, process ('autoresponder').

Three very good companies that offer this service include AWeber Communications (**aweber.com**), MailChimp (**mailchimp.com**) and iContact (**icontact.com**). AWeber is a very popular autoresponder service which, at the time of writing, has more than 80,000 customers. It is a paid service that starts from around $19 per month. You can however opt for a trial period if you want to take your time to discover what will work best for you. AWeber is reliable, flexible and comes with plenty of training and support. The service also includes functions for data distribution, reporting, testing of email campaigns and analysing campaigns.

I have used autoresponders within my own email marketing on my blog **ihubbusiness.co.uk**. When visitors subscribe, they are sent an automatic, emailed, welcome message by our autoresponder service, which requires them to 'opt-in' to further emails from us, and also lets them know that we will be sending them a series of tips on internet marketing over seven days, two free eBooks to download and regular email updates thereafter. At the end of each email there is a link for people who choose to unsubscribe. All this is fully automated, saving me a great deal of time and keeping my end of the bargain to boot (i.e. their details in exchange for the above gifts).

The system I use, **icontact.com**, like AWeber, has excellent video tutorials on how to set up an autoresponder. It is free up to a certain volume of subscribers and offers a number of additional features, such as analytics and enabling the sending of information to social media sites.

Your email employment system needs to provide, as a minimum, the following metrics in a standard report upon the completion of an email campaign. These metrics are as follows:

- The percentage delivered
- The bounce rate (%)
- The open rate (%)
- The CTR (click-through rate %)
- The number of recipients who opted out.

How to succeed with email marketing

If you are selling products on your site, then 'triggered' emails will significantly help boost your conversion rate. Triggered emails are simply emails which are 'triggered' in response to customer behaviour. You will need to invest in good software to realise the huge potential in this area; at the end of this section I include some well-regarded providers.

According to Carolyne Nye, Marketing Manager of S&S Worldwide, (a 100-year-old direct marketer of arts and crafts, sporting goods and educational supplies), 40% of all the company's email-generated revenue comes from triggered and transactional-based emails that account for only 4% of the total email volume. This is an incredible return on investment. Nye recommends a range of 'triggered emails' including:

Welcome email

A welcome email is your site's opportunity for a personal communication with the customers. "Wow them with the benefits they'll receive as subscribers, give them information on the frequency they can expect contact information, and, possibly, a new subscriber bonus of some kind," says Nye.

Example:

Dear Helen Ross,

Thank you for signing up to receive the Learn and Play newsletter and great email savings! As a subscriber, you will receive exclusive email notification of our special sales and offers designed just for people like you! In addition, the following are some of the many benefits available for you at www.mywebsitename.org.

You can:

- Check the status of your order online
- Request a catalogue
- Discover great tips and resources in our free online resource centre
- Browse for discounts and offers in our seconds section
- And more!

Our popular emails are sent out on the first Monday of every month, so look out for it. Each email promises to be jam-packed with tips and tricks to entertain even the most resistant of children!

Do get in touch if we can be of any further assistance to you.

Best wishes,

Emily Harper
Customer Care, Learn and Play

☎: COMPANY TELEPHONE NUMBER
@ : COMPANY EMAIL ADDRESS

Reorder or order reminder emails

Depending on your business model and the frequency of customer orders, you may want to trigger a message based on the customer's previous orders. For example, several of S&S's customers tend to order similar products once every year. They receive an email at the 11 month mark, which includes all the information from their past orders, making it easy for them to see what it was they ordered and if they would be interested in ordering the same or similar products. This email is very effective for any replenishment-type product.

Example:

Dear Helen Ross,

We noticed your interest in our Gobi bear products which you purchased on xx/xx/xx. It is our pleasure to offer you £10 off your next internet order, irrespective of what you choose to purchase, valid until xx/xx/xx. To claim your discount simply enter the promotional code xxxx when prompted to at the checkout.

To order different items simply click here **www.mywebsitename.org** to start your shopping!

LOGO HERE
COMPANY DETAILS

Birthday or special-occasion emails

According to Nye, if it makes business sense for your site to capture subscribers' birthdays, email them to say "Happy Birthday" and include a special offer. The logic here can also apply to any other date-driven event.

Abandoned cart emails

In Nye's view, this is one of the more powerful emails in a marketer's tool box. It reminds the customer that they have selected items from your site to put into their online cart, but never reached the checkout stage. Some ecommerce sites have been wary of sending abandoned cart emails for fear the consumer may feel overly monitored. However, in practice, most retailers find that the customers value the reminders as a great service. Once set up, abandoned cart emails can run automatically and they will help capture lost sales. Test the timing, message content and product offers in these emails to find the combination that best works for your site. Companies such as **www.seewhy.com** specialise in technology to assist with abandoned cart programmes. Customers have already credited the product as being useful enough to want to purchase them. It could be that they had wanted to come back to the purchase and had forgotten to do so, or had changed their minds. Either way curiosity for something which is personal to them will spur on the opening of the email.

Transactional emails

Transactional emails are a form of triggered email since they happen automatically following an online order. They provide an opportunity to create and maintain a lasting relationship and to encourage repeat purchases. They tend to have the highest open rates of any other email within a programme. What's more, customers tend to keep these particular email communications in their inboxes for a longer period of time. This means, as a retailer, you can use these communications as an opportunity to remarket. An ideal series of transactional emails can include some of the following types:

- Order acknowledgement/confirmation
- Order processing notice
- Shipment notification
- Follow-up customer service survey
- Request to review products bought

Nye's five keys to transactional emailing success

1. Include relevant customer service and order information. Include details of a customer's order and shipment. Also, include a way for the customer to contact your company regarding his or her order.

2. Link back to your site. Include a way for customers to return to your site. Perhaps frame the link in your top or side navigation.

3. Encourage social networking. When your customer has just placed an order, he or she would may want to share the experience with others. Make it easy for customers to share their thoughts with others by linking to social networking and bookmarking sites. (I discuss this more later in this chapter, and in Chapter 7.)

4. Encourage future purchases. Transactional emails are a great place to promote special offers, rewards programmes or refer-a-friend programmes.

5. Include up-sell/cross-sell items. Many leading ecommerce sites include in their transactional emails personalised recommendations that are dynamically rendered based on the customer's order or browsing behaviour.

Emailing best practices

Your database

The single most important measure for your email campaign is sheer deliverability. If your email does not make it past the filtering of either your recipient or of their internet service provider, it has zero chance of being looked at.

You really must have opted-in addresses, as this is crucial to deliverability. It is equally important to make it easy for your customers to opt-out of your emails. Let people know exactly what they will receive from you and how often.

The Direct Marketing Association Email Marketing Council produces Best Practice Guidelines which should help to steer you through these waters. Visit **www.dma.org.uk**.

A good tip is to set up a routine, e.g. monthly, to remove from your lists any names that bounce back as undeliverable. If too many names are listed as undeliverable, an Internet Service Provider (ISP) may label you as a spammer. It takes even fewer spam complaints to an ISP to put you on a 'blocked' list.

Your subject line

The first words that will be seen by your customers are the words within the subject line. It is therefore absolutely fundamental to make sure that your subject line is clear and compelling, with the promise of value to come, leading to a desired action – however small that may be. There are blogs which are devoted in their entirety to the art of crafting a 'killer' headline or title. And for good reason. This is your chance to be read!

Below is a chart showing the Open Rate for US Email Marketing Campaigns by Subject Line Content, March 2010. The response is based on one, three and seven days from when email was sent.

	1 day	3 days	7 days
Abandon cart	84%	95%	99%
Welcomes	76%	91%	97%
Offer	79%	92%	98%
Time-limited offer	79%	93%	98%
Free shipment	81%	93%	98%
Coupon	76%	91%	98%

Source: Experian Cheetah Mail, provided to eMarketer (www.emarketer.com)

If people are in the market for those products which the email relates to, it will spur them towards a quick response.

The key is to put benefits into your subject line rather than a pushy sales message. Subject lines should be no more than 45 characters in length. An example of a good subject line could be:

- BRIGHTWORLD – Act Fast! Brightworld's 4 Hour Sale Bonanza Starts Today.

- Zineb Fatmi – New Arrivals: Vermeil bracelets make the ultimate iconic statement.

Your "from" field

It is good practice to use your company's name so that your email has credibility. This also ensures you maintain your email reputation as an online business.

Make sure that you have good legislative adherence – e.g. anti-spam compliance. The Privacy and Electronic Communications Regulations are the rules that dictate how you perform your online marketing, such as by email. Sites such as **www.gov.uk/data-protection-your-business** will help you. You can also familiarise yourself with data quality essentials at **www.ico.gov.uk** to avoid being blacklisted by firms whose job is to find emailers that are not compliant. Using a reputable email provider will ensure that you minimise the chances of this happening.

Internet service providers set up 'honey-pot' addresses that are aimed at catching spammers. They will also keep track of the servers they suspect of sending spam and will block these servers, so it is important to choose a solid email provider. If you have names that you are manually adding to your database, be sure to test those names first in a test mailing, to ensure they are deliverable.

Personalise your emails

Make sure your emails use the appropriate level of formality or informality for your customers. Sending a corporate, stuffy email to a young, laid-back readership is unlikely to work!

Message body

Your message must include a call to action, even if that is encouraging the reader to click through to your website or another site, or to fill in a survey or questionnaire. The case study which follows this section should give you some insights and tips for message content success.

Irrelevancy is the new spam. It takes just a few badly targeted or badly personalised emails for your emails to start getting ignored. Think of your subscribers as individuals, rather than an amorphous bunch of email addresses you can push your sales messages out to, and you will notice huge improvements in your campaigns.

Tip

Ask for profile and preference information when people sign up and opt in. Look at purchase data, both offline and online, to get an idea of their preferences. You could also look at your analytics to see which emails have been responded to and which have prompted action. This information should help you to build up a picture of the individuals who are getting your emails and what interests those individuals. As your subscriber base increases you will most definitely require the ability to segment your readership, in order to craft emails that are of interest, relevance and value to them.

Footer section

Currently, legislation requires that all emails contain an accurate physical address. The footer is a good place to put this. You should also consider the following elements for the footer part of your emails:

- A reminder of when and why readers are being written to – e.g. Consider a "Why was I added?" link, to remind subscribers when they opted in to your emails.
- Email address the message was sent to.

- Privacy Policy link.

- Contact number and/or customer service details.

- Unsubscribe link or a 'Manage my subscription' link.

Optimise your emails for social media

Social sharing prompts, asking readers to connect on platforms such as Google+, Twitter or Facebook, can improve exposure for your message and help you build up your database. I can recommend **share.lockerz.com** which will allow you to download the Add-to-any button, for free.

Emailing X-factors

Offer opportunities for people to opt-in to your mailing list from every page of your website. Make sure you provide something of value to motivate people to sign up, for example a free eBook or a free sample. Internet users surveyed by Exact Target said that they give an address mainly for the promise of discounts and freebies (Source: **www.emarketer.com** – original source Exact Target "Email X-Factors", 24 June 2010).

Embrace new sign-ups authentically and enthusiastically. A quick autoresponder generated welcome email is all you need to confirm a new relationship has begun, as described above.

Make sure you have your logo on your emails. Write with one authentic voice and with your brand's personality in mind. This will require some thought, as you will need to be consistent in your tone and approach – people will not trust a Jekyll and Hyde correspondence! A great example of a consistent email voice is the Daily Candy. The emails look like pretty stationery and now there is an app for the New York market, sending mobile editorial content alerts to Android users whenever they are geo-located near a sale or deal it recommends. Throughout, the emails retain the femininity and playfulness that is now synonymous with the brand.

Work out the best times to send your emails. Pure Research analysed more than 660,000 emails sent by 34 companies, and discovered that the volume of marketing emails opened dropped significantly during the lunch hour. Only 9% of the emails sent were opened between noon and 2pm, with 62% of those opened being news or magazine alerts rather than promotions on goods or services. Using the research, Pure 360's team identified patterns in consumers' responses to different email marketing promotions throughout the day including the following useful insights:

- The Abbys (10pm to 9am) – the worst time to send email.

- Working Late (5pm to 7pm) – here there is a significant rise in recipients opening holiday promotions during this period, it is also when business buyers have time to find out about Business to Business promotions and so forth.

- Last Orders (7pm to 10pm) – recipients are more likely to respond to consumer promotions in their own time; offers on clothes and special interests, such as sports and gym promotions, perform very well during this time period.

Make sure your emails are relevant. The way to do this is to pay particular attention to your customers' purchasing behaviour and profile them well. For example, I am frequently sent emails by Amazon based on purchases I have made over a period of time, and presented with email alerts for new products either by the same maker, line extensions or promotions related to products I have already bought. Do not make the mistake of sending promotional email alerts to customers based on one-off purchases they have made however, as they may not appreciate this, and might even choose to opt-out of your future correspondences. Instead, study behaviour over time and plan your campaigns accordingly. My autoresponder email provider enables me to segment my customers, which makes it easy to send out targeted emails and autoresponders.

Use coupons. Coupons and discount vouchers are a major driver of consumer behaviour, especially in times of recession and economic difficulty. Instead of offering coupons or discount vouchers to everyone in your list, offer them selectively so that you can maximise engagement or re-engagement where you most need to. Coupons can drive a discount ladder, whereby you present the most aggressive offer to those who have been least responsive or have longer inactivity. It works. In the course of my research for this book, I joined an American 'Making Money Online' scheme that applied this technique. The idea was to persuade me to spend around $100 dollars on the 'system' which had been 'sold' through a series of webinars, emails, testimonials and presentations. My lack of response noted, I was offered entry into the scheme for $50. In other words, a 50% discount to buy my subscription and potential as a long-term customer. And yes, of course it worked! Here is a summary of how it works:

- Give higher markdowns to those least likely to respond.
- Lower markdowns to those most likely to respond.
- Reduce markdowns even more for those likely to spend anyway.

Stick to a consistent frequency schedule. Consistent communication is the basis of any relationship. However, do not bombard; ask your customers how often they would like to hear from you. What is important is that you do not waste your time by 'checking in' with your customers; only send information they will value. Examples of information you can send to your list fairly frequently include:

- News of upcoming events – e.g. sales
- Tips and tricks for your industry or product – e.g. to save time, money, effort or resources
- Daily digests of industry news or updates
- Monthly newsletters.

Make your call to action compelling and clear. I have visited many a website where it is unclear what I am being asked to do. Use arrows or buttons to make it easy for your customer to take action to make a purchase. If you are sending an image of a latest product, embed the link to where customers can purchase that product within it.

Optimise for mobiles. The rise of smartphones means that your email is likely to be read on smaller screens, so make sure that it can be read easily off a mobile phone or tablet. A good rule of thumb is to keep your email below 20kb for mobiles.

Each device will display your email differently, so find out which mobile devices are popular amongst your customers and design templates optimised for those devices. Tools such as Veracity Mailbox IQ can provide you with this level of information; visit their site for more information. Have a look at how your emails look on a variety of phones. Optimising for mobile is crucial – I access 90% of my emails on my smartphone.

Integrate your email with social media. Social media is comprised of a wide range of internet-based, word-of-mouth forums including, but not limited to, the following:

- Social networking sites, such as Facebook or LinkedIn
- Content-sharing sites, such as Flickr, YouTube or Pinterest
- Micro blogging sites, such as Twitter
- Blogs – both individually and company-sponsored
- Collaborative projects, such as Wikipedia
- Social bookmarking sites allowing users to recommend online sources, such as Digg or Reddit
- Virtual social worlds, such as the spookily named Second Life.

One of the essential factors about social media platforms is that they are primarily engagement platforms. When you integrate your email with social media, you can choose whether your emails will be shared on any of your social media engagement platforms.

Tips for integrating your email with social media

- Place calls to action in your email messages.

- Good email provider systems will ask you if you wish to add social sharing buttons to your emails, and also buttons to enable people to sign up for your Facebook page or become a Twitter follower.

- Identify advocates of your brand on social media and recruit them as 'brand champions/advocates'.

A recent report from the well-respected eMarketer, entitled "Brand Advocates: Scaling Social Media Word-of-Mouth", has highlighted the growth of brand advocacy over the last five years and also provides tips on how businesses can cultivate brand advocates, as well as how to avoid annoying those who support your brand. You can read more of the article at **www.emarketer.com/Article.aspx?R=1009074&ecid=a6506033675d47f88165 1943c21c5ed4.**

Why brand advocates are good for business

- They frequently recommend products and services. A Zuberance study (**www.emarketer.com/Article/Brand-Advocates-Here-Help/1009074**) found that over a third of brand advocates recommend a brand once a month, while 12% do so several times a week.

- They educate others on how and why to use a product. Brand advocates will usually write about brands to offer advice and support to others.

- Brand advocates tend to interact with brands and consumers on brand/company pages. They actively take part in companies' online activities. This suggests a useful strategy may be to find ways to target these brand advocates beyond just Facebook likes or Twitter mentions.

How to recognise brand advocates

eMarketer suggests that there are eight attributes businesses can use to recognise brand advocates:

1. They are usually, but not always, young.

2. Your brand advocates could also be mums and dads. In other words, do not make the mistake of assuming they are always young or technologically conversant. It is a good idea to cultivate all potential advocates across demographics and sectors.

3. They are helpful to others. However, it is important to note that the strength of voice brand advocates usually enjoy within their circles of influence can either work for you or against you.

4. They want their favourite brands to succeed. Think of ways to help these advocates spread the word about your success.

5. They are active offline, too. Therefore, think of ways to tie your online marketing campaigns into your offline campaigns and vice versa.

6. They feel a personal connection to brands. Find ways to feed this connection such as "Virtual Manager for a Day" or similar.

7. They use social media more than the average consumer.

8. They are influenced by social media.

What is the best way to reach, engage and cultivate brand advocates?

There is no rule book guidance on this, however an effective strategy is to work out how different groups respond to different promotions and communications, and develop distinct campaigns for each group. Once it is clear that some individuals are more responsive to your campaigns than others, involve them more in your campaigns; seek out their opinions and demonstrate the value you place on their input. You could also consider offering your brand advocates discounts or incentives based on their referrals or brand advocacy.

Measure the success of your email campaign

The most common way to measure the success of your email campaign is by calculating your 'open rates'. This is expressed as a percentage and calculated like this:

Open rate = Emails opened ÷ emails sent – emails that have bounced

So a 60% open rate would mean that 6 out of 10 emails delivered were opened up. The measure is not perfect, but it gives you an idea of how successful your emails have been. Here are some things to bear in mind:

- Relevance is important. The less segmented your email list, the lower your open rate is likely to be.

- If your audiences are very busy you will experience lower open rates.

- Niche topics, e.g. homeopathy, tend to have higher open rates.

Case Study: How to write emails that give you no choice but to read on

This case study comes courtesy of Robert Clay, one of the UK's leading marketers. To have a look at his blog, visit **www.marketingwizdom.com** where you will also have access to his well regarded book: *Learn how to grow your business… in just two hours: introductions to low risk/high-return marketing strategies that will help you transform your business.*

America's number one sales authority Jeffrey Gitomer recently wrote a widely syndicated article about an email he received from Robert Clay of Marketing Wizdom.

Here is what was written by Gitomer:

"I got an unsolicited email this morning that gave me no choice but to read it. My interest had to do with the subject line, the headline, the design of the content, and the copy.

The subject line was: *Jeffrey, How to go from market penetration to domination.* Ok, I clicked to open.

Then the headline: *What one thing determines your success in business, more than any other single factor?* Ok, I read it. The very tastefully designed letter said:

'Hello Jeffrey,

This is Robert Clay.

If you were asked what one thing determines your success in business more than any other single factor, what would you answer?

Perhaps you'd say it was down to the quality of your product or service, or your people, or trust, or competitive prices, or availability, or profitability, or the number of customers who return to do business with you again.

These are the responses I get all the time. While they're all good answers, the biggest factor that determines your success in the marketplace is one that is hardly ever written or spoken about … and in ten years not one person, out of the thousands I've asked, has been able to tell me what it is.

Perhaps you've heard me speaking on the subject in the past, or read about it in my book. The point is, once you know that one factor that makes a world of difference, you can take a few simple steps to move your business from market penetration to market domination.

Just look at Google who now have 85% of the global search engine market; and Apple, now the world's most valuable technology company, who dominate the market for music players, smartphones, computers priced over £600, and now tablet computers too.

When times are tough you REALLY need to work smart. You need to do what Google, Apple and others have done. You need to know that one factor that can change everything for you.

That factor is explained in my book on page 10. And you're welcome to download a copy with my compliments, with absolutely no obligation. Just click here, enter your name and email address, click the confirm link on the email you receive and you'll be taken to a page where you can download the book immediately.

If you enjoy the book, let me know. If what you learn leads to the transformation of your business, as it has for some, then be sure to let me know!

Click here to get your copy of my book, with my compliments.

Warmest Wishes,

Robert Clay

Marketing Wizdom Ltd'

Ok, I clicked, subscribed and downloaded the free book, and immediately went to page 10 to find the answer… Eh, not so fast. That's not what this lesson is about. The point of this article is for you to see what Robert Clay's writing was about, what got me to "click" and most important, how can you use these same elements in your communications – both as email cold calls, and email follow-ups.

The object of an email is NOT to get it opened and read. The object of an email is to get RESPONSE. A positive response.

Here are the "buttons" Robert Clay pushed to make me "click here" to get the free report and the answer to his headline question:

- He asked me provocative questions.

- He made me curious.

- The letter had value-driven engagement.

- The message had perceived value to me as a reader.

- The letter had a free "hook" offer that promised "value-first."

- The letter had NO offer or obligation to buy anything.

- Clay offered new information.

- Clay offered success information.

- The letter offered something about or for ME!

- The letter had the lure of an "answer" about something I want.

- The letter met a now-need that I have (timing of the message). I want to know this, or have this, NOW.

The reason I'm sharing this information is not to prove a point, or even to provide an "AHA." I'm giving you this information and challenging you to take a close look at the way you send emails, and the way they are responded to (or not).

Now that you have seen what makes me click, why not study what makes your customers and prospective customers click. What's their button? What answers are they looking for? Where's your value?

Or are you just "checking in" or "touching base," making a feeble (and obvious) attempt at trolling for dollars?

In today's world, you have no choice but to be seen, known, and perceived as a person of value if you want to differentiate yourself, make the sale, and build the relationship.

Every sales oriented email you send should answer the question, "Where's the value?"

Credibility factors that encourage people to buy

On the internet, trust is hard won and easily lost. Thanks to the vast rise in email spam, credit-card fraud and spyware, customers are becoming increasingly cautious of whom they chose to do business with. However, there are a few steps you can take to increase your credibility and trust.

Online security

Ecommerce: If you are using PayPal or WorldPay to process transactions, your users' credit card details will not be stored on your server, but on the very secure servers of those service providers each of whom has policies to protect customers from fraud. Include the logo of your reputable provider prominently to reassure your visitors, on your website and on your landing pages. Another sensible step is to link to the providers' consumer protection policy pages. To do this requires some basic knowledge of HTML; I suggest you ask your web developer or designer to show you how this is done, and where to place the link. It is also important to ask your designer or developer make sure the link opens in a new window or tab, so they do not navigate completely away from your site when they visit the supplier's site.

Make sure your Privacy Policy and Terms and Conditions have been thoroughly drafted by a lawyer and ensure these pages are easy to navigate to.

Accreditation

Consider joining organisations such as SafeBuy (**www.safebuy.org.uk**) to demonstrate your commitment to your buyers' security and safety. Again, display the logo prominently on your website.

Email

As you will be storing the email addresses of those who sign up, using a licensed autoresponder service and adhering to anti-spam regulations will help you ensure that the customers' details remain on your system.

Make sure you notify the Information Commissioner's Office (**www.ico.gov.uk/for_organisations/data_protection/notification.aspx**) that you will be storing personal data.

Social proof

Conduct regular customer satisfaction surveys. Ask your customers. Ask them what they value most about your service or do not value. In addition, obtain basic information from them, such as their age and gender which can give you powerful insights such as the characteristics of those who buy particular products or services. Let your customers know through the survey that you will be using their comments on your website, whilst reassuring them that their full name will not be visible. Be sure to only use the positive comments! Social proof amounts to a vote by the people for the worth – or lack of worth – of something. Therefore, the more endorsement others see from real people, the more likely they are to trust you.

Quick summary

- Build relationships with your customers and they will stay loyal to you.
- Use permission based marketing systems as best practice.
- Follow emailing best practices to get your emails read.

Chapter 7
Social Media

To be effective with internet marketing you need more than just your website. Social media has grown into a powerful marketing channel in its own right. At the time of writing, 78% of internet users conduct product research online, and almost half of all daily internet searches are for information on products and services.

Source: www.flickr.com/photos/brantleydavidson

In this chapter you will learn:

- What social media is.
- What social media marketing is and how to decide which social media platforms to use for your brand.
- How to market to the three "biggies": Facebook, Twitter, and LinkedIn.
- Best practice tips for online PR.
- How to track your social media progress with a WordPress blog.
- Social media case studies.

What is social media?

To refresh your mind, the term social media refers to a variety of sources of online information which has been created, shared and used by individuals such as you and me. Social media is made up of a wide range of internet-based, word-of-mouth forums, including:

- Social networking sites, such as LinkedIn, which I discuss later on in this chapter.
- Content-sharing sites, such as Flickr and Pinterest.
- Collaborative projects, such as Wikipedia.
- Microblogging sites, such as Twitter, which I discuss later on in this chapter.
- Social bookmarking sites which allow individuals to recommend other sites, such as Digg or Reddit.
- Virtual social worlds such as Second Life.

Social media is one of the most popular ways of disseminating and seeking information. They are seen by people as being less biased than traditional advertising and it is for this reason that social media is so popular with marketers. Social media will facilitate:

1. **Conversations with your customers**. You can use platforms such as blogs and social networking sites to share product details, list benefits, announce promotions, etc. With social media you can present a message to a very targeted demographic and see if your message resonates with your customers enough for you to use it as your primary medium of marketing. For example, if your product or service is targeted at young customers, you could try Facebook which is very popular with younger age groups.

2. **Your customers talking to one another**. Social media allow one person to communicate with tens of thousands of people about products and services, instantly. This is described as 'going viral'.

To be successful it is important for you to learn not only where and how your customers gather information, but also how you can leverage the conversations about your brand that are being had. How? By joining in!

What is social media marketing?

Internet marketing authority David Meerman's explanation of social media marketing is one of the most accessible I have come across:

- You can buy attention (*advertising*).
- You can beg for attention from the media (*PR*).
- You can bug people one-at-a-time to get attention (*sales*).
- Or you can earn attention by creating something entertaining and useful for others and then publishing it online for free: a YouTube video, a blog, a research report, photos, an eBook or a Facebook page (*social media marketing*).

The platforms you use should reflect where your customers "hang out", although as already mentioned, there are some benefits in being on multiple channels. Each platform also brings its own characteristics, for example:

- Currently on Facebook the largest demographic group is the female, 18-25 age group – but the average age on Facebook is 38. Top interests are communities, fashion and cosmetics, politics, instant messenger, humour and discussion.
- On Twitter the average age is 39 and popular tweets centre on politics, fashion and cosmetics, science and nature, humour, news and information, and then instant messenger – in order of importance. You are limited to 140 characters per tweet.

LinkedIn is widely regarded as the professional's business networking site, and the average user age here is 44.

YouTube is one of the highest trafficked sites, with well over 2 billon views a day. The audience is split equally between males and females and the overwhelming majority of visitors are from outside the USA.

How to market on Facebook, Twitter and LinkedIn

Facebook (www.facebook.com)

If you are new to Facebook, a good starting point is to read up/learn about how it works and the benefits a Facebook page can bring to your business. Here are some good starting points:

- Facebook page creation: (**www.youtube.com/watch?v=wlbLOfvgMWI**)
- Facebook fundamentals for business: (**www.youtube.com/watch?v=bEOLVi3nzh8**)

A Facebook Business Page is a great way to supplement your website. You can include everything from company location and contact information, to updates and videos.

Pages also track the number of likes your business has achieved. Just as individuals have their own accounts on Facebook, businesses do too. You will need an account on Facebook in order to create and maintain a business account on Facebook. Having more than one Facebook business account is a violation of Facebook's Terms of Use.

Opposite is a screenshot of the Facebook page of one of my favourite cupcake stores, Lola's Cupcakes:

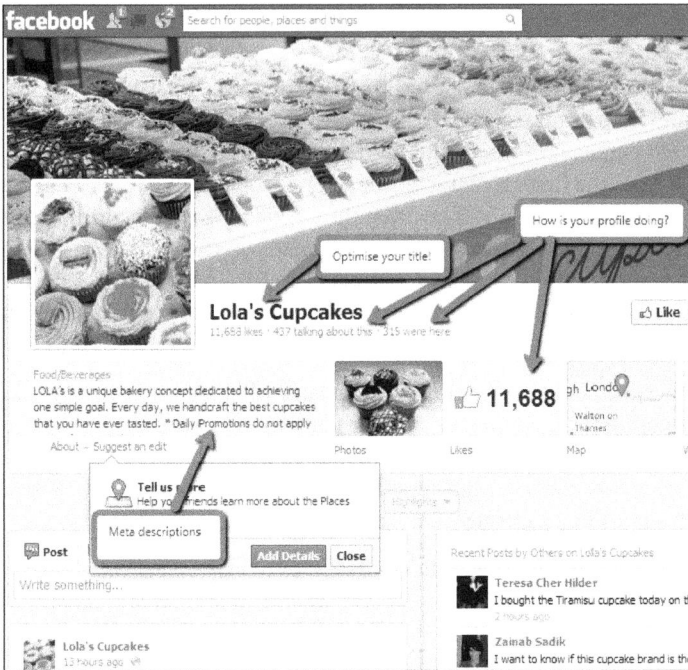

Let's begin by exploring the important elements.

SEO Title: Your Page Name | Facebook

Building up a brand is very important in social media, so it is important to make sure that the title of your business page reflects your brand. This is especially so if you want people to be able to find you under by brand name.

Meta Description: Your Page Name + Your About Description | Facebook

Make sure you write a great, keyword rich Meta Description for your brand. To edit your About information to make a great Meta Description, go to your page and Edit Page > Basic Information, and fill in the About field with a 140 character description that reflects your brands, value proposition, i.e. the value your brand offers captured succinctly using relevant keywords.

Optimising your fan page updates to promote good search engine rankings

Each of the status updates on your Facebook fan page have a page of their own (click the timestamp of one to see). If you're posting a standard update on your wall, the search engine optimised Title for the individual page of your updates will be pulled from the first 18 characters or so of the update. If you're posting a link to your fan page wall, you will be given the option to "Say something about this link…" – the first 18 characters of what you enter in this field are going to be the search engine optimised Title of that status update. What does this mean? Well, in a nutshell, keywords. Make sure you include your keywords in the first 18 characters of your update!

If you're concerned about optimising your updates while considering them as individual pages under the umbrella of your fan page, then you might want to consider placing some keywords at the start your comment. For example, if you are posting an update about vanilla cupcakes, just start the update with 'Vanilla cupcakes'. This is a simple, effective way to keyword optimise each update.

Once you have your page created, follow these steps to help you get started:

1: Develop a game plan and strategy

There are three important goals to aim for in your Facebook marketing:

1. **Increasing Your Engagement**: Engagement and/or interaction are critical as they are the means by which subscribers, fans or followers can be 'nurtured' into advocates of your brand. Engaging with others will keep your profile updated often, and if you are helpful to your followers it will lead to others recommending you to their audience. A very important goal!

2. **Increasing Facebook 'Likes'**: Many small businesses feel this aspect of Facebook is 'too pushy' and therefore ignore it. This is not advisable, as the whole 'liking' aspect is key to both getting others to do your marketing for you (often referred to as 'social proof') and also building your subscriber database, and therefore prospect lists. The practice of getting someone to 'like' your Facebook page does not seem culturally 'very British' given our natural, or learned, reserve, however, it is important to develop more of a 'this is marketing' mentality and work with the culture, not against it.

3. **Increasing Sales**: This is, of course, your ultimate goal. Being liked and having great interaction with your community is all well and good, but

you still need 'calls to action' to ensure that something happens, the bills get paid and you can take care of your family!

2. Use a custom tab application

Companies such as **ShortStack.com** will enable you to create custom tabs, i.e. customised Facebook pages, with an aesthetic and functionality boasted by the pages of big businesses, either for free at their basic plan or at a fraction of the cost. It really is a "piece of cake"; no programming know-how is needed. If you are struggling however, I suggest you go straight on to YouTube and search for ShortStack videos at **www.youtube.com/user/ShortStackLab**, where you will be guided through, step by step, how to use the application. These pages have a variety of uses; for example, you could create a landing page as your welcome page – encouraging 'likes' – that is highly visible to your visitors. You could use a custom tab to announce special discounts or sale.

Post videos and images on your page, to the extent even of a gallery of your products. You can customise your content so that it appears selectively to fans or non-fans. The software allows integration with Google Analytics, so you can track your key performance indicators. Currently, this feature is with the paid option, but is well worth the small monthly investment.

3. Increase engagement

Engagement through interaction is very much part of the 'Facebook culture'. If you are using a custom tab application, such as the ShortStack application, you will very easily be able to run promotional features, including contests, and sweepstakes with virtual gifts, e.g. a 'limited edition' ebook. A good video that will walk you through how to run contests on Facebook using ShortStack is **www.jonloomer.com/2012/04/30/how-to-run-a-facebook-contest-with-shortstack**.

Custom tab applications, such as ShortStack, will also make it very easy for you to run polls, publish news, post videos, images and much more.

Facebook is a visually-driven medium, so take advantage of these tools. They will help people see the personal aspect of your brand. Photos of events, people using your products, and your team, are all examples of the photos you could use.

Respond to comments and posts on your wall from your customers in a timely fashion, as this is a source of feedback from your customers. Even if the feedback is not positive, take this as a chance to demonstrate your commitment to resolving customer issues swiftly.

Leverage the 'real time' aspect of Facebook. Do you want to announce a time-bound sale for unsold items – for example, one that will be over within 24 hours? Post it on your wall! A good tactic is to post a discount coupon for your fans to print off and bring into your store. Instil a sense of urgency by making it time-bound.

Social media is not for everyone. If you have placed yourself in that camp, then there are alternative ways of managing this very important internet space. For example, you could outsource key elements of your social media strategy to freelancers or companies. If you enter "social media consultant" into Google, you will doubtless be presented with an abundance of choice. A good tip is to seek out recommendations from others who you know have worked with social media consultants.

4. Make sales

In the same way as the discount coupon, create a voucher that needs to be printed off and brought into your store to receive further advantages, such as a discount on your product or service.

Twitter

www.twitter.com

Twitter is a very valuable business tool that can achieve a number of different objectives, from responding quickly to a customer complaint to announcing a contest. For businesses and brands, Twitter enables you to take part in conversations about your industry, niche or brand. Twitter is a great way for you to share (or 'tweet') helpful information to your 'followers' and participate in conversations to drive your desired actions forward. Businesses use Twitter to listen and gather market intelligence and insights – it is very likely that people are already talking about either your industry or niche, your brand or your competitors.

The basics

Twitter, I'm afraid, comes with its own language which you will have to get to grips with. Fortunately this is unlikely to take you long.

The first thing to learn about Twitter is that it allows you to send – or tweet – messages within a strict maximum limit of 140 characters. Here are the basics to get you started:

Mention: Once you have signed up to Twitter and chosen your username, you and anyone else can mention an account in your tweets (your messages) by preceding it with the symbol @. For example; "I am so glad you enjoyed our scrummy bouja chocolates @joeking!"

Retweet: If you come across a tweet that you want to share with others in your community, you can do so simply by clicking 'retweet' below it to forward it to your followers instantly.

Message: If you want to send a private tweet to a user who is already one of your followers, you can do so by preceding your tweet with 'DM'. This is called a direct message. For example; "DM@joeking what is your tracking number for the parcel?"

Hashtag: You will come across the very popular hashtag, a # symbol which people on Twitter use within their messages to categorise them for other people. For example; "Have a look at our new exotic chocolate line for Christmas http://t.co/mylink333 #exoticchocs." Hashtags are best thought of as a way of identifying a theme. Users can then click on the hashhtag to see other similar-themed tweets and hopefully yours too!

For a good walk through Twitter terminology go to:
support.twitter.com/articles/166337-the-twitter-glossary

For now though, you have the basics. What about your Twitter profile? Below is a screenshot of what your Twitter profile will look like once you have followed the simple joining instructions:

Profile image

With your profile image, make sure you optimise it – i.e. make it easy for the search engines to pick it up – by using your name as the filename. Twitter will use your name under the profile settings as the ALT tag for your profile image as well. In Twitter your user name (i.e. your chosen @name) and your name are used as the title tags in your profile (see Chapter 4 if you need a refresher on the importance and use of title tags).

Although not shown on the profile image above, when you write your bio as part of the process of joining Twitter, make sure you include your keywords. Important services such as Klout, which is a service that grades the influence of people on Twitter, and other Twitter search engines use the keywords in your bio in the search results when people are looking for similar folk to follow. You can also include a link in your bio, if you wish.

How to get the most from Twitter

Find customers for products

You can search for tweets about your products and your niche in general. As people will tweet all manner of content, from their frustrations to their joys, a good search on Twitter will give you insights into the keywords used by customers, and also what the customer likes and does not like. If you have found customers who are looking for what you have, you can then interact with them, follow them, and nurture their custom.

Build your brand's credibility

Twitter can help establish your reputation through the quality of your tweets. Provide useful updates, share valuable links and insights, and you will soon become known as a trusted source of information. There are Twitter question and answer tools such as **inboxq.com**, which enable you to answer questions and show off your expertise.

Customer service

Twitter is a great and flexible channel to demonstrate the quality of your customer service. People on the internet are not backwards about coming forwards with their complaints and issues. They will tweet about their problems and the service they have received. If your company is nimble enough and flexible enough to respond, in a way that exceeds the customer's expectations, you are on to a winner. This sort of rapid response is what builds customer loyalty and trust.

Build a following

Success on Twitter is very much a matter of achieving a critical mass of followers. This should be a goal, although a 'large number' is one which will have to be decided by you, based on your competition for instance, who similarly have Twitter followers. Building up a large, relevant following is not easy to achieve, but it can be done and there are tools that help ease the process. The big secret to making a success of Twitter is down to the quality of your content. Tweet often, tweet high quality and original content, tweet add-value information, interesting information and hot news; retweet others generously, link to external information, add media. These are all great practices that will help raise your profile on the Twitter sphere.

Top tips for Twitter

- Start off by writing around 100 quality tweets before you search for others to follow.

- To find people to follow, search on Twitter for keywords that relate to your niche. Find the most interesting tweets that come up through your search and check out their profiles. If you like what you read, follow them.

- Pay attention to what it is about their tweets that attracts you and try to incorporate elements of this in your own tweets.

- It is also a good idea to check the number of tweets they have sent out themselves, because if they have only written a handful, the chances are that they are using automated software and will therefore be very unlikely to engage with you.

- The more active you are on Twitter, the more success you will have and this includes being an authentic follower yourself, as well as encouraging others to follow you.

- Share content that your followers and potential followers will find valuable. For example, a successful business I work with shares photos and behind the scenes information about her baking business.

- Regularly monitor the comments about your brand, competitors, products or your industry.

- Ask questions to engage your followers and glean insights from what they say.

- Respond to positive comments with a simple "thank you".

- Regularly tweet information about special offers, discounts and time-bound deals.

- Demonstrate your expertise in your area. Share links that are relevant, quote experts, etc.

- Champion your supporters. Retweet them and reply publically to compliments from others about your business. Remember that Twitter is, in effect, a free marketing tool so take advantage of it!

Useful resources

You can use the Promoted Accounts featured in Twitter to quickly build a critical mass of loyal followers. These are used for several reasons, such as:

- Getting known quickly.
- Building up to a product launch/line extension.
- Capitalising on a particular 'hot' event when a Promoted Account will be most relevant.

Building a strong base of engaged Twitter followers should be one of your key goals Twitter followers who spread your messsage are instrumental in helping your business take off. Following on Twitter is a very strong indication of online affinity. This is because the people who are following you have indicated enough of an interest in your brand.

Promoted Accounts are shown in the search results and also within Twitter's 'Who To Follow' section. This is Twitter's account recommendation tool which identifies like-minded accounts and followers to help users discover new businesses and people on Twitter. Your Promoted Account appears in this section for users who have been identified as most likely to have interests similar to your account. To find out more about promoted acounts visit: **business.twitter.com/en/advertise/promoted-accounts**

There are many tools that will help you organise and manage and track your interactions with Twitter. Some of these tools will enable you to schedule your tweets for dates in the future, such as the Buffer tool which I use. Others will shorten very long links for you, and others will even suggest people for you to follow on Twitter. Here are my top five tools:

1. Bit.ly (**bitly.com**)
2. Buffer (**bufferapp.com**)
3. **HootSuite.com**
4. **Socialoomph.com**
5. **SharedBy.com**

Let's go through each briefly to see what they offer, but I do suggest you learn more by clicking through to the sites themselves.

Bit.ly: A free **Bit.ly** account will give you access to a dashboard where you can shorten and share links to multiple Twitter accounts. As an added bonus, you can even create your own custom short domain to match your brand, so you can have branding similar to Amazon's *amzn.to* custom URLs.

Buffer: Buffer has described itself as "A smarter way to share" and I have to agree. It enables you to simply schedule your tweets to be spread throughout the day/week/months so you do not have to go through a reading spree and inundate your followers with 20 tweets within an hour. Buffer also gives you information on your numbers, your analytics, regarding your tweets. This will help determine what your audience values, or not, from the content you share, as well as the times of day you get the most action on your tweets.

HootSuite.com HootSuite comes with a free plan for those who have fewer than five social media profiles to manage. HootSuite allows you to connect to multiple social networks from one website. HootSuite can help you use social media to launch your marketing campaigns, identify and grow your audience, and distribute targeted messages across multiple social media channels.

SocialOomph: SocialOomph is a useful service that allows you to schedule tweets, track keywords, extend your Twitter profile, and much more with an unlimited amount of accounts for free.

SharedBy: SharedBy lets you create a custom sharing bar. This custom share bar will typically include your name and social sharing icons, as well as links to your website. It can even include a Tweet button which recommends your Twitter accounts, as well as a Facebook Like button that connects to your Facebook business page. It can be installed on your blog for outgoing links, and installed as a bookmarklet on your browser bookmark toolbar as a quick way to share with your customisation at the top of every link! This really is a very useful tool, and I suggest you head over to the website to understand in greater detail how it works.

Bonus Tool: Twitter Search – quite literally the search box in Twitter – is a very effective monitoring and research tool. You can follow hashtags, chats, and what people are saying about your company/competitors.

LinkedIn

www.linkedin.com

Why use LinkedIn?

LinkedIn is often regarded by those not too familiar with it as a social networking site for high powered businessmen. This is a misguided view. Rather, LinkedIn is an online network of influential people all over the world. For most people, gaining contact with the most powerful people in business is one of their biggest challenges. LinkedIn essentially brings business people together, online. I am very far away from being a CEO of a multinational company, in spite of this, thanks to LinkedIn, I now have relationships with some pretty influential CEOs from some sizeable multinationals. The point is that, utilised properly, LinkedIn can allow even the humble baker's assistant to engage in discussion and build connections with company CEOs. Having experts in your niche within your reach can only be beneficial to your business. If you manage to build a good relationship with them on LinkedIn, who knows, they may be willing to endorse your product or perhaps engage in an interview with you on a relevant subject, and if they agree, you could then publish the interview on your website.

LinkedIn can help you find business partners, clients and service providers

LinkedIn can assist you in building a network of useful contacts. Simple searches in your field will reveal thousands of experts, service providers and potential clients. If you do not personally know an individual, you may request to be introduced through a mutual contact or can send an introductory email.

LinkedIn is a good blog promotion tool

If you or your business has a regularly updated blog, LinkedIn is a great way to share and promote it. LinkedIn allows you to add a blog or website link (simply click on the '**Edit profile**' and write your details there) to your individual profile in order to give it exposure.

LinkedIn for recommendations

The LinkedIn recommendations feature is also very useful. Once you have added products or services to your company profile, you can request recommendations from your customers. Recommendations are a powerful way to boost your business' credibility and gain new clients.

LinkedIn to improve your search engine results rankings

LinkedIn allows you to make your profile information available for search engines to index. Since LinkedIn profiles are well received by Google from a search rankings point of view, this is a good way to influence what people see when they search for you or your business. It is key to make sure your profile is as search engine friendly as possible.

Below is a screenshot of my brother's LinkedIn profile, showing the following important elements of a LinkedIn profile:

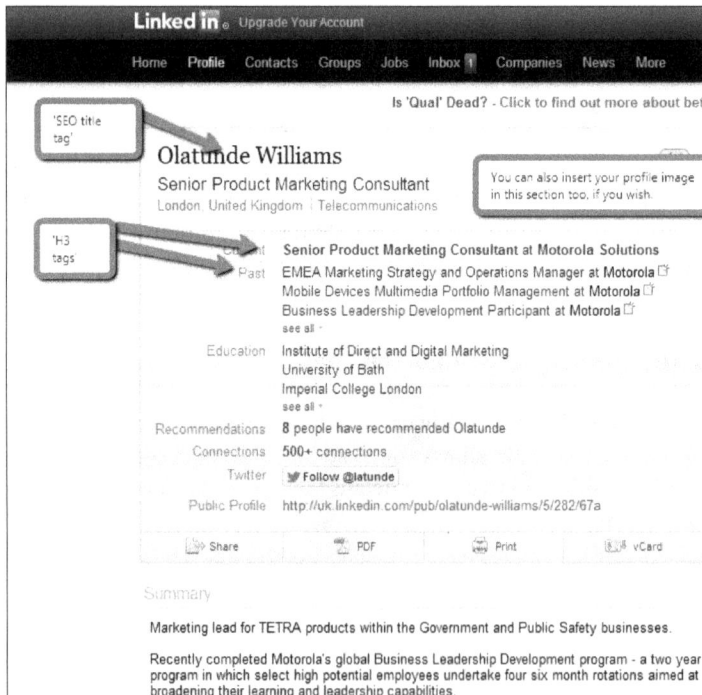

Profile image: the filename of the image and your name as the ALT tag

You will need to use your name as the filename for your profile image – if you are unsure of how to do this you will need to ask your web developer/designer. LinkedIn will use your name as the ALT tag for your image as well (refer back to chapter four if you need a refresher on tags).

Job titles: H3 tags

Your job titles or your area of expertise belongs in this section. To give yourself a good chance of ranking well in the search engine results, make sure you get some keywords in here. For example, if your business sells vermeil jewellery and you are an expert in this field, your 'job descriptions' could include keywords such as 'Vermeil jewellery retailer', 'Expert on vermeil jewellery', etc.

According to LinkedIn expert Lewis Howes, to rank well for keywords searched within LinkedIn's people search, you will need to include your targeted keywords in the following areas:

- Your professional headline
- Summary
- Specialties
- Skills.

I would also suggest joining some industry appropriate groups, which are then automatically publicly listed on your profile and can add to extra keyword usage on your profile. To learn more about groups visit **learn.linkedin.com/groups**.

Tips

- For a great read on how to use LinkedIn groups to build influential connections, go to:
  www.socialmediaexaminer.com/5-ways-to-use-linkedin-groups-to-build-influential-connection
- You can add your portfolio or even a video to your LinkedIn profile. All you do is set up a free **Slideshare.net** account and upload your presentation or video there. Once this is added and enabled to your profile, you can copy the code you are given and paste it onto your LinkedIn profile page.

Resources

Connect your business website or blog to LinkedIn. The LinkedIn share button lets users share your website with their own LinkedIn connections. This will in turn drive traffic back to your site. Go to **developer.linkedin.com/plugins/share-button** and you will soon be on your way!

Best practice for online PR

The power of media editorial for shaping customers' opinions of their products and companies continues unabated. What has changed is the way in which marketers go about gaining that editorial coverage online. How can you use the internet to create a buzz around your own products and services?

In my days as a magazine editor, I would be inundated with requests from journalists who had targeted my publication on behalf of their clients, to get favourable coverage of products or services. Sometimes this happened through well written press releases, other times I would be pitched original, interesting articles or ideas.

Whilst this type of PR still exists, the rise of the internet has added a new dimension to the media, and has created many new opportunities to gain coverage. Here are three significant developments:

1. Emailed press releases are now the norm, and online services such as Response Source – which helps connect journalists and spokespeople –

are common place, however companies are now also using social media tools, such as Twitter, to contact journalists.

2. Online versions of publications are now expected, particularly with the increase in the use of smartphones. Or, people are reading blogs and interacting with friends and strangers in online forums and other social media platforms. This has meant that companies are increasingly targeting bloggers who they believe are influential in their space, as well as online journalists. For example, influential bloggers are introduced to sponsored events, broadcasts and support programmes; the idea being to provide information in an informal setting, free of the constraints and commercial styling of traditional PR. Get it right and your company or product can feature on a blog that has more readers than a daily newspaper, and which also has the ability to make content go viral. Blogs are perceived as being less biased than traditional media, less corporate and therefore more credible.

3. The world has changed. The post-recession marketing landscape is digital. Conversations are online. There are an overwhelming number of companies who are using the new social framework to reach out to customers, whether that is through digital campaigns or customer relations channel. Now it is about online reputation, and taking a more one-to-one approach with influential journalists. Identify the most relevant journalist and attract them with information that they will want to know. Rather than 'Public Relations', online PR is 'Personal Relations'.

A great way to get more publicity for your business is to use an online press release distribution service. Three of the best ones are PRWeb, Business Wire and Market Wire and they will all have their own specifications on how you should submit a press release to them. These services will distribute your press releases with the advantage to you of giving your business a broader reach. These services will have access to bloggers, journalists and prospects that are beyond your email list. Here are six ideas for the types of content you can generate for your press releases:

1. An award or accomplishment that your business has achieved. An online press release can take the story beyond your industry and connect you to influential people, such as journalists and bloggers in your niche.

2. An award your suppliers have won. The implication? You sell award-winning products/services.

3. An event you are organising. You can tease out different aspects of the event including, but not limited to, the speakers, the content, the attendees, etc.

4. A charitable contribution you have made. Not only will this generate awareness and credibility to the cause you believe in, it will also generate positive publicity for your business and connect you to others who believe in the same cause.

5. Share interesting statistics, results from studies or recent research. Put your best stats forward and show people why they should care.

6. Provide helpful hints on how to use your product or service. "How to" types of content are very poplar – type 'How to' into the Google Keyword tool to see just how popular these searches are. If you are selling computers then you could, for example, write a list of keyboard shortcuts. Or, if you are selling gold jewellery you could write a guide to the worth of carats of gold.

Contacting and interacting with journalists on Twitter

You could, of course, contact journalists directly. How? Search in Google for 'Journalists on Twitter', or use directories such as Wefollow (**www.wefollow.com**) to locate journalists in your space.

Tips

- Find a journalist or blogger who echoes your own values and follow them on Twitter, Facebook, etc. Show you value their content by retweeting information of value and commenting favourably on their tweets. It is important to do this over a consistent time period – be patient!

- Make sure you are comfortable enough with your information so you are not 'stumped' when asked for a comment.

The Dos and Don'ts of Twitter PR

- Do not send a direct message to journalists with a selling pitch. Good journalists are not interested in sales pitches, even less interested if they do not have a relationship with you. They have plenty of relationships already. What good journalists are looking for is high quality information that is relevant to them. Keep your tweets about your expertise as it is relevant to them and avoid tweeting information that is in nobody's interest but yours. You want to keep your journalists on side, and avoid the risk of them 'unfollowing' you or ignoring your tweets.

- Avoid the temptation to tweet lots of tweets in a row. This would be frowned upon at best, at worst your reputation would suffer as you will be thought of as a spammer.

- Do respond to journalists who are following you back in order to introduce yourself – developing the relationship is important and this is an opportunity to do so. In time you could also ask the journalist to introduce you to a specific journalist if he or she is able to. Referrals go a long way!

- Do send an @message to journalists asking if they would be interested in the press release or story that is relevant to their needs. There should be a clear value to them in receiving this press release. Doing this gives you a way to build rapport and relationships. Keep in mind that they all will see if you contact multiple journalists through @messages. So you need to decide if you want to be desperate or focused.

- Do not contact a journalist multiple times on Twitter. If you haven't heard anything in a few days, then follow up with an email or a phone call and mention that you first tried on Twitter.

- Do give them some information on a topic when they put out a 'request for information' tweet and regularly monitor the #journorequest tweets.

- Do say thank you when they do write about the idea you put forward to them. Look out for story ideas for them, especially if they are good follow-up stories for ones they've already written.

- Thank them for covering an event you attended, especially if you were able to chat with the reporter. Touches like this will help them remember you and ease the development of the relationship with them.

- Monitor and post your tweets with hash tags on your town and topic – for a great read about using hash tags to market your business read this post: **blog.hubspot.com/blog/tabid/6307/bid/32497/How-to-Use-Hashtags-on-Twitter-A-Simple-Guide-for-Marketers.aspx**

Tip

Set up 'Google Alerts' for online PR case studies at **www.google.co.uk/alerts** – it will take you about a minute to do this – (see screenshot below). Setting up this alert will direct you to real life examples of how others have done it! It is also worth setting up an alert for your own business so you can track how your online presence is developing by the number of mentions you get.

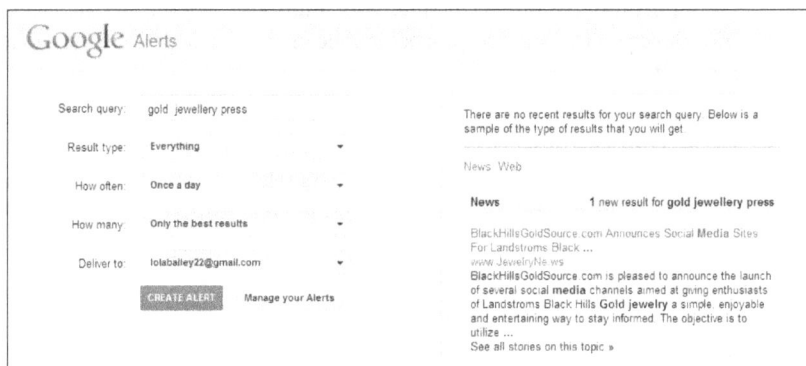

How to track your social media progress with a WordPress blog

As I hope the chapter on Google Analytics will have taught you, it is important to keep a track of your performance numbers so that you can evaluate your progress and think about what you need to do differently to improve.

Social Metrics is a WordPress plug-in which helps you analyse the social response on your blog.

A plug-in is a piece of hardware or software that adds a specific feature or service to a larger system, such as a website or blog. The idea is that the new component simply *plugs in* to the existing system. WordPress has a large range of plug-ins you can browse. A comprehensive list of these is at the back of the book.

Social Metrics is not a free tool, however you are offered a 60-day 'full money back guarantee' if for any reason you are not happy with it.

With the help of Social Metrics you can track which of your posts perform best in terms of social media exposure. To download it visit **wordpress.org/extend/plugins/social-metrics**.

If needed, ask your web developer/designer to help you install the plug-in. After successful installation and activation of this plug-in, click on the Social Metrics link in the left sidebar of your dashboard. You will be taken to settings section of Social Metrics. Everything should be self-explanatory from this point onwards.

Key features:

- You can track how your content is shared on the main social media channels, including Twitter, Facebook and LinkedIn.
- You can find out exactly how many times your posts/pages have been shared across these social networks.
- The performance of all blog posts and pages is helpfully displayed in tabular format.
- You can use this information to find out which of the social media sites you should concentrate your efforts on.
- You can access Social Metrics from your WordPress dashboard.
- You can effortlessly share posts/pages over the social networks from right within the Social Metrics Dashboard.
- Social Metrics is a lightweight plug-in with minimal settings.

To learn more about Social Metrics visit the main website at **www.socialmetricspro.com**.

Social media case studies

Activia

Activia launched a Facebook campaign targeting women aged between 20 and 50 in April 2010. The main goal was to bring the brand closer to the consumers and develop brand awareness, focusing on the Activia drink product. This was achieved by asking consumers to compete in five different challenges through different stages. The campaign was mostly online, while one final challenge extended to a small offline event. Promotions were supported by television and point of sale terminals and created a big buzz.

Users posted pictures of themselves with Activia products and spread the word. The main prize went to an organised trekking trip to Indonesia, climbing a 3726m high volcano. She reported back by writing blog posts every few days, so others could follow and see the whole great experience. With the right engagement, the brand become more searched, more shared, developing a 52% increase in branded search and a 620% increase in referring page views; not to mention word of mouth communication.

Blendtec

The company uses Google Analytics to track its traffic from social sites, but also analyses other metrics – such as the conversion rate of shoppers who click through and the percentage of shoppers who use coupon codes shared on a social network – to get a sense of whether its social media efforts are leading to sales.

Blendtec also focuses on measuring sales that result from exchanges on Facebook. After an initial Facebook Like, for instance, the manufacturer engages with consumers by providing information, such as additional giveaways, or highlighted features of its new products, or a recipe for cranberry sauce it posted just before Thanksgiving. To account for the sales that result from consumers entering its contests, the retailer gives shoppers unique coupon codes which are tracked upon redemption.

Blendtec's social marketing campaign fits with the manufacturer's other marketing efforts, which are largely focused around branding.

Quick summary

- Social media should be integrated into your marketing plan.

- Find out where your customers are and make sure you are there too.

- Use available free resources to help you start strong.

- Don't go for a 'hard sell' on social media – that's not what it's about.

- Track your progress on the main sites based on what you have decided you want to achieve for each – here is a brief summary with some suggestions of what to track:

  - **Twitter**: Are your Twitter follower numbers increasing? Are your tweets being shared? Are they being saved by people in their 'favourites' menu? Are they being retweeted by others? Are your links getting clicked on? Tools such as Bufferapp or HootSuite, Social Oomph or even Twitter Search will help you find out.

  - **Facebook**: Is your fan base growing? Are others 'talking about your brand' as shown on your Facebook page? Are your contests/polls proving to be popular? Are people using your coupons or vouchers? More importantly, have your sales increased, compared to a previous period? Custom tab applications, such as the aforementioned ShortStack, allow integration with Google Analytics, so you can track your key performance indicators.

  - **LinkedIn**: Are your LinkedIn connections increasing? Are you connecting with relevant influencial people in your niche?

  - **Online PR**: Are you and/or your brand getting positive mentions/reviews online? Have you seen more traffic to your site following any press releases you have sent out? Use tools such as Google Alerts or Social Oomph to track the mentions your brand is receiving; from whom, why and the context of the mention.

Chapter 8
Building For Long-term Success – Affiliate Marketing

In this chapter you will find out:

- How to set up an affiliate marketing programme.
- How to successfully implement your affiliate marketing programme.
- Useful affiliate marketing resources.

What is affiliate marketing?

Essentially, affiliate marketing is a performance-based marketing channel. It is a great way to increase sales and broaden your reach, without spending a lot of money. Think of your affiliates as a virtual sales team.

Affiliates are people who can drive traffic, preferably qualified consumers, from websites, social media platforms, and PPC marketing to the retailer's site.

How to set up an affiliate marketing programme

There are two ways to run an affiliate programme. You can set it up and manage it yourself, or you can work with one of the affiliate networks.

Do it yourself

There are advantages to independence. Joining a network can be very expensive. The benefit of setting up your own network is the ability to control all aspects of the network, including campaign management. If you set up your own network you do not have to worry about a third party having visibility into your programme, and you can avoid being affected by third party policy-changes which can potentially have an effect on your business.

For this option you will need to purchase affiliate software, which will track your affiliate sales and enable your affiliates to view their stats. If you are opting for the DIY approach you will have to work hard to find the best affiliates.

Finding affiliates to sell your products

The first and most obvious way to recruit affiliates is to create a new page on your website, advertising the fact that you have an affiliate scheme. A straight forward 'Become an affiliate' call to action should do, but make sure you clearly explain how to join your scheme and the benefits of joining your fair and generous affiliate scheme. Optimise your page for your niche/keyword, e.g. "Golf products affliate programme". Make sure that your title tags, meta descriptions header tags, ALT and image tags, which I have already discussed in Chapter 4, are all reflecting your keywords for your scheme, so that affiliates can easily find you through a quick Google search. This on its own will not be enough, however. You should also:

- Advertise on affiliate forums such as **www.abestweb.com**.

- Make sure your programme is listed in Affiliate Programme Directories (simply type 'affiliate programme directory' into Google).

- Join and actively network on affiliate forums (type 'affiliate forums' into Google).

These should be your priority 'to dos' when looking for affiliates. They will of course require time and commitment on your part. Do make friends in the affiliate world and you will be rewarded with great information that will undoubtedly be your useful for affiliate programme. Making friends in itself requires commitment, which is why, when you do join an affiliate forum, make sure it is one you are happy to be consistently active on. How do you find the right forum? Well, this will be for you to decide. Dip your toes in a few and then settle for the one which you feel has the quality of affiliates you are happy to interact with. Better still, seek out those who have experience of independent affiliate programmes and ask for their suggestions.

There are other activities you should do to locate the best affiliates for your programme and make contact with them:

- Go onto YouTube, and look for active affiliates or those with popular video channels in your niche.

- Video sites are very popular 'hang-out' sites for affiliates, so YouTube is a good place to visit.

- Search for your niche and your niche products and see what comes up. If it seems to you that there are high quality videos selling products that are not their own, the chances are these are affiliates.

- Start to build a relationship with the ones that have impressed you by virtue of their understanding of the products and also their communication of the benefits of the products.

- Demonstrate your expertise in your niche, too. Gradually you will start to build a relationship based on mutual respect and appreciation. This is a good basis for making an approach. Google places a high ranking value on social media sites, so you want affiliates who have a strong YouTube profile with their own channel.

- Search is going social, so you want fresh affiliates with video presence and/or strong social media skills. Twitter is also a great place to try. Go to Twitter and use **twitter.com/search** to perform searches on your keyword phrases, your product/site names, and your competition.

- Listen out for people who are already talking about your niche or your niche's products. These are the people who are interested enough in your target market to talk about it. The chances are, they would welcome the opportunity to make money from these products too.

When you do make contact with the affiliates you are interested in, bear in mind that the best ones are usually very busy – as you would expect. You will be given very limited time/space in which to get your message either read by them or ignored.

Tips

- Approach them wherever you find them. If the conversation is one that is clearly enthusing them, that would be a good time to make contact. If you find their blog, contact them through their requested method of contact – usually a contact form. If they offer a number, pick up the phone and call.

- Get to know them before you send a message to them as discussed above. Address them by name. Include something personal, such as an article they have written recently and which you perhaps can offer some further insight on.

- Keep your messages to the KISS principle, i.e. short n' simple.

- Bear in mind that fundamentally, affiliates are marketers and can see through deliberate sales pitches. Relate to them as fellow marketers. Keep their interests at the forefront of your mind. For example, approach them with an offer, e.g. a coupon code that will be of interest to their readers and explain why.

- Make sure you only approach affiliates who are already working within your industry. The best affiliates will not appreciate random requests – this will be a waste of both your time and theirs.

- Do not spam them with communication; for example do not send a tweet, followed by a Facebook comment, a blog comment, a phone call and a voice mail all within the same day. They will avoid you like the plague.

- Give them an extra incentive to work with you; for example, an exclusive interview with one of your LinkedIn contacts you have recently made! Other enticements could include a very generous commission rate or a coupon.

- Do let them know that you are interested in working with them personally, on the basis of the evidence you have seen to date, e.g. articles they have written, videos they have made, mentions of them in social media, etc. Flattery, if genuine, i.e. based on fact, can work wonders.

How does the reader gain the initial contact with the affiliates if they are opting for the DIY approach?

There are however limitations of the DIY approach to having your own affiliate scheme. Some affiliates could be wary of independent schemes. Many fold after a short period of time; after the affiliate has invested much effort into promoting the products and services. Also, affiliates are generally put off by having to keep track of several independent schemes when they could get all of their statistics from one network source. Networks will also aggregate payments from different advertisers so affiliates reach their payment threshold sooner.

Furthermore, you will be solely responsible for setting up and maintaining the network, recruiting affiliates, establishing and enforcing policies, and managing payments to your affiliates. Monitoring fraud will also fall to you. Fraudulent practices to be aware of include click fraud (caused by the deliberate automated inflation of clicks on an advert, for the purpose of causing a charge to the advertiser), and re-bill schemes that lure consumers into "free trials" that result in one or more unwanted subscriptions. Other practices include redirecting traffic to a fraudulent web address. To minimise the risk of fraud consider investing in tools such as **www.directtrack.com**.

Joining a network

Examples of popular affiliate networks include AffiliateFuture (**uk.affiliatefuture.com**), Deal Group Media (**www.dgm2.com**), TradeDoubler (**www.tradedoubler.co.uk**), Netklix (**www.netklix.com**) and Paid on Results (**www.paidonresults.com**).

Affiliate networks will provide all the reporting tools; they will also track sales and pay affiliates on your behalf. Crucially though, they bring companies operating affiliate programmes (also called advertisers or merchants) together with potential partners – affiliates (also called publishers). By joining Affiliate Window (**uk.affiliatewindow.com/homepage/about-us**), for example, you gain access to 40,000 active UK affiliates.

The cost of using networks

As well as a setup fee and monthly charges, networks usually charge a percentage of the money paid to affiliates, called an override. How does this work? Imagine an affiliate generated a sale for you that was worth, say, £100. If you are paying your affiliates 10% commission, £10 would go to the affiliate and the override of, say, 30% of that would go to the network. Therefore you would pay £13 for the sale. Costs of using networks are generally quite high but they do vary and most of them will negotiate with you.

Questions to ask before joining an affiliate network as a merchant

It is important that you ask the right questions of any potential partner. Below is a list of suggested questions you may consider asking; it is important to retain the element of control – it's your business!

- How many UK affiliates do you have?
- How much does it cost to join your network? Are there any extra charges, e.g. ongoing fees?
- Can I interview the affiliates before I agree to them joining my programme?
- How do you assess the effectiveness of affiliates?
- Can I offer different commission structures to my affiliates?
- Does your network allow spyware? *Spyware products should be a warning flag for you to stay away. These products are associated with scams that are damaging both for advertisers and publishers. Spyware sits on a computer and intervenes when the user visits an advertiser's site, inserting the spyware's affiliate code. Any affiliate that referred the visitor loses the commission, and the advertiser can end up paying for visitors to its website, even if they just type in the address. Spyware can be particularly hard to tackle for advertisers administering their own programmes.*
- Do you support text links and banner adverts?
- Can I communicate directly with my affiliates?
- Will you help me recruit affiliates?
- Will you give me advice on adverts?

Treat your affiliates well

Whichever route you go down, experienced affiliates will want to liaise with someone who is 'at the helm', someone who has the power to make changes, get things done, change processes. This will be you, or if your budget permits, someone who you have appointed as an affiliate manager. It is important to spend time building relationships with your affiliates; keep them on side and on board with your programme.

How to successfully implement your affiliate marketing programme

The most important factor for success is having great products that people want to buy. It is also important that your website is one that is clearly successful. It is easy to suggest numbers; for example, some would suggest you need a minimum of 500 unique visitors a day to your site. However, you also need a site that is credible, trustworthy, and which has been well designed to attract visitors.

A good metric to monitor is the number of affiliates actually driving traffic. A healthy, active affiliate programme generally has about 30% of their affiliates driving traffic at any given time during normal working hours. This percentage should hold true no matter how large the programme.

To keep your affiliates motivated, set up an opt-in list to enable them to subscribe and receive new promotional methods, sales letters and articles to assist them in making more sales. This will not only increase their sales, but it will also enable you to keep in contact with your affiliates and introduce new products. It is best practice to keep your communication with your affiliates to a consistent level – whilst there is a line not to be crossed in terms of personal intrusion, it is better to over-communicate rather than under-communicate with them. Add a 'personal' touch to your emails too; share a story if it relates to the topic of your communication, or a signature sign-off at the end of each communication are simple actions you can take.

Seek feedback openly from your affiliates. What should you keep on doing? What should you do more of? Less of? Differently? You can do this via a simple survey online or by email. Not only does this demonstrate your commitment to them, it can also be a nice way to learn more about their business and professional goals or objectives for the year ahead.

The key to obtaining affiliates is to offer a very generous commission for each sale. There are at least two options:

1. **Percentages**: A percentage pay scale is easy for your affiliates to digest – the bigger the price tag, the more they make. This type of commission structure can work well for you if the same holds true for your company; after the cost of goods sold, the bigger the price tag, the more you make.

2. **Flat Rate**: A flat rate commission will work well for you if your profit after cost of goods sold is roughly the same across the board. In other words, if you aren't making considerably more by selling higher priced items, then neither should your affiliates.

The higher the commissions, the more affiliates you will recruit. Some websites offer in excess of 40% commissions to their affiliates. You will need to do some research on the going rate in your sector as a starting point. Try and match this, if possible. Successful, hardworking affiliates will move to another company that offers them more reward if you do not give them adequate recompense. Consider the lifetime value of a customer when working out what you can afford to pay. In some very competitive niches, advertisers will pay more than their margin on their first sale because they are confident they will make more from each customer in the long term.

After an affiliate is approved, they should get access to the retailer's advertising inventory. If you have a banner advert that is already proving to be successful, then use this as a starting point. Generally speaking though, the popularity of banner ads is waning. Banner adverts are almost invisible now that internet users are experienced at screening them out. Effective advertising tends not to look like advertising. A good example would be a review of a product or service followed by a couple of paragraphs explaining the features and benefits, and then a link to the product using a 'click here to receive our launch discount'. These tend to work best as the user does not necessarily think that they are being sold to. Internet users are generally sceptical of being sold to, so a more subtle approach is required.

Provide your affiliates with a range of links in different sizes, colours and designs. Experienced affiliates will know what works best and it is also better to have too much than too little. Text links are very effective, so as I have just touched on, enable your affiliates to link to your products directly. Affiliates also prefer unbranded creatives and will avoid adverts that make it easy for customers to conduct business without going through their link. This is seen as an attempt by the business owner to use them as 'free branding'. Instead, go for creatives that do not include the merchant URL or the merchant telephone number. The idea is for prospective customers to click on the affiliate link and not bypass this link by clicking on the merchant URL instead.

Analyse your results using the reporting tools at your disposal. Identify your most successful affiliates and work hard to keep them motivated. Monitor adverts for both click-through and conversions. It is worth pointing out however that you can have low click-through rates but high conversion rates and you will not want to reject these adverts. Share what you know with your affiliates – be transparent; for example, let them see which creatives are performing well and which ones are not.

Promote your affiliate programme on a site, such as AffiliateAnnounce (**www.affiliateannounce.com**).

Useful affiliate marketing resources

- JROX.COM Affiliate Manager (**www.jam.jrox.com**) is an affiliate management software system which will help you set up your own affiliate scheme. The software is designed to help you recruit, manage and build your team of affiliates who can then help you promote your products or services (for a generous commission). There is a free version and a paid version. The free version is exactly the same as the licensed version, except that it is limited to 50 affiliate members.

- MyAP.com (**www.myaffiliateprogram.com**) is a well-respected system that can also help you to set up your own affiliate network. The software will allow you to segment your affiliates based on your chosen characteristics, and it also simplifies the commissions process, click-through pages and linking methods, such as:

  - **Banners**: The software will generate banners in a variety of sizes to fit tops of pages, bottoms, toolbars, sidebars and other miscellaneous areas.

- **Articles**: These are helpful for affiliates who prefer or need more content for their websites and newsletters.

- **Email Ads**: Your affiliates may be interested in placing adverts in their own newsletters. In MyAP you can generate a few advertisements in different lengths.

- **Signature Files**: Some of your affiliates may even add your tag to their signature line. Give them a few options to choose from.

- **Guestbook**: Provide your affiliates with a guestbook, which in turn will help you build your opt-in email lists. Offer them a commission for each email address they send you, or a proportion of the revenue from any purchases that the subscribers they send you make.

- **Product Images**: Give your affiliates images that show and link directly to specific products. Let them choose an image specific to their site, or choose several images to display.

- AssocTRAC (**www.assoctrac.com**) is an affiliate tracking software that features real-time tracking of statistics. It tracks both visitors and sales for each associate, to determine not only the quality of visitors, but also if your advertisement is converting visitors into purchasers. It includes an easy sign-up process that instantly creates accounts for associates, so they can be up and running very quickly. An auto-responder email message is instantly sent out with linking instructions and other detailed information. This powerful software tracks through the use of cookies and CGI scripts.

Chapter 9

Planning for the Future – Optimising for Mobile

Marketers took little notice of mobiles until the launch of the iPhone, which made mobile marketing a necessary reality. This in turn accelerated the development of the smartphone market, giving many people the technologies – without the expense – to access the mobile web.

Source: www.flickr.com/photos/dave_fisher

In this chapter you will learn:

- Why you should take mobile seriously: five mobile commerce and engagement statistics.
- The benefits of mobile technology.
- Ways to use mobile phones as marketing tools.
- How to be successful in mobile marketing.

Why take mobile seriously? Five important statistics for mobile

1. 40% of British consumers using a smartphone while shopping made a purchase either in-store, online or via a mobile. (Source: eDigital Research and IMRG Survey, 2011.)

2. 33% of UK shoppers who have seen a QR code have scanned one. (Source: eDigital Research and IMRG Survey, 2011.)

3. As many as 91% of UK consumers have used their mobile device for commerce, to either research or purchase a product. (Source: Global Consumer Survey from MEF, 2011.)

4. 50% of UK smartphone owners report shopping from their mobile device, and 11% of these do so on a weekly basis. (Source: Portaltech and eDigitalResearch, 2011.)

5. By 2013, mobile internet sales is expected to reach as much as £275m, 4% of online retail spending, up from £123m in 2010. (Verdict & Ovum, 2010.)

Benefits of mobile technology

Cost: Compared with the cost of production, printing and delivering direct mail, mobile marketing is relatively inexpensive. At the time of writing, a straightforward SMS marketing campaign costs just a few pence per text sent.

Always on: We will happily turn off our radios and TVs, and we will speed past billboards. But our phones? They stay on pretty much all of the time.

Data capture: Mobile campaigns are well placed to obtain data about their users. It is very easy for users to key in and send information on their location, gender, age, sex, etc.

Portability: You can link your campaigns to specific locations by having a Bluetooth message or an SMS sent to people within a certain radius, thereby driving footfall to a shop, restaurant, etc.

Control: You can deliver your message to a specific number and so you know who will receive your message. This means you can tailor your communications with a high degree of accuracy.

And some facts:

At the time of writing, the following statistics are true of mobiles (Source: eDialog 2011, Nielsen 2011, eMarketer 2012).

- 56% of smartphone users say email marketing strategies have become more relevant to them in the last 12 months.
- 45% of web mobile use is spent checking email.
- 23% of all email is read on mobile devices.
- 77 billion mobile app downloads are forecasted for 2014.

As people are becoming more comfortable with new technology, the expectations will be for content to be:

- On every device
- Consistent across platforms
- Relevant to the platform.

Mobiles enable us to have better access to information, real-time access to that information and importantly, real-time content sharing across social platforms. Indeed, for the first time since the invention of TV, people are watching less of it – particularly the aged 18-25 demographic.

Using mobile phones as marketing tools

Optimise your website for mobile

Services, such as those provided by Duda Mobile (**www.dudamobile.com**), offer free and paid services to help you optimise your website for mobile, offering one-click conversion, the ability to customise your site and synchronise with your regular website. To synchronise, or sync, means to compare at least two sets of data and make them match each other. When you sync your iPhone or other device with a second device – such as your computer – the process will cause both devices to contain the same data, such as photos, music, addresses, etc.

Identify and understand your mobile audience

Understanding the demographics and preferences of your mobile clients, and how they use their devices, is a critical first step in finding out what will appeal to them as useful and unique. The first question is whether your targets use conventional feature phones or smartphones, such as iPhone, Blackberry or Android. The more sophisticated the device, the more sophisticated your messages will need to be. It is also worth considering how you are currently interacting with your customers, in terms of frequency, of contact and of tone.

Take advantage of precise targeting to make the best use of your mobile channel

Mobile marketing can be a double-edged sword. On the one side, you have a highly effective marketing channel that boasts significant advantages over other advertising and marketing channels; on the other side, you have an extremely personal interface which means you could alienate the very people you are seeking to attract. Mobile platforms now have the ability to collect user data on both location and preference, to store this information in a database, and to create real-time campaigns, segmented by interests, around specific themes. It is not unusual to hear of mobile advertising networks reporting click-through rates that exceed those on the desktop web by a factor of more than ten. All the more reason then, to make sure you deliver highly relevant, useful messages. More and more mobile phones are incorporating global positioning satellite (GPS) technology, giving you valuable information about where your customers are. Think about how you can use location in your campaigns to deliver the right message, at the right time (i.e. not in the middle of the night!).

It is also vital to make sure that you follow a policy of opt-in, permission-based, marketing principles.

Leverage SMS (text messaging)

Whilst there are lots of opportunities to deliver your content directly through the phone via, for example, apps, you can also use the phone as a messaging device to alert your customers about your content on your other platforms, such as your YouTube channel or your own branded Facebook page. 8 trillion SMS text messages were sent worldwide in 2011. SMS boasts the highest open rates across messaging platforms, and it is easy to see why.

Here are some uses for SMS:

- Increase traffic to your website – send reminders and promotions.

- Boost brand engagement – send alerts about special offers and activities.

- Enhancements – mobile only benefits.

- Mobile couponing – a text message containing a coupon is sent to a customer that can be redeemed in store or online by entering a code.

A Harris Interactive study, 'The Alert Shopper 11: Consumer Receptivity to Location-Based Marketing' (2 July 2010), found that among the mobile users who signed up to receive text alerts, 34% said they would be more likely to visit the company's website in response to the alert, and 33% indicated that they would visit a physical store.

Location based services

As I have touched on, more and more phones – indeed most smartphones – come with a GPS receiver embedded in them and this offers marketers great potential. GPS technology can provide marketers with highly significant data, which can enable them to present relevant offers and rewards, right when customers are at the point of decision making! When customers have entered a shop with their mobile phones, for example, product information or coupons can be instantly delivered to them.

One restaurant I recently read about in the US uses geo-location very successfully. The restaurant uses the Foursquare geo-location application to retain its customers through rewards, such as special discounts tied to the number of their visits. A customer who checks in to one of the restaurants five times, for example, will see an offer pop up on their phone for a dish served by the restaurant. These customers are not only likely to remain loyal, but if the quality of the restaurant is good to boot, they will probably become advocates and tell others. As cited in a *New York Times* article, published 6 October 2011, 1,400 people checked into the restaurant a total of 2,800 times.

Influence your mobile customer's pre-purchase decisions

Mobile shoppers rely on their devices to help them make a variety of purchasing decisions, ranging from where to shop, to what products to buy. To increase your chances of success, here are some steps you can take:

1. Ensure your business is listed, and strategically advertise on all major local sites, including Yelp, Google Places, Yahoo Local, Qype, etc.

2. Make sure all your print, internet and Yellow Pages listings are correct.

3. Mobile shoppers compare product prices, and look for coupons and deals, making it clear that price is a major determining factor in predicting sales. In the past, the availability of pricing information was limited, unless customers scoured through newspaper ads or travelled between shops. Small businesses today need to take a closer look at the online marketplace, to determine the average prices of products they sell, and adapt their own prices as best they can to be more in line with other retailers. Alternatively, small businesses can make clear in their mobile advertising why buying from their shop at higher prices has added benefits (more experienced staff, savings on shipping, immediate availability, better customer service, longer warranties, better deals for bulk purchases, etc.).

4. Local businesses should also look into posting coupons on their social media channels, featuring daily deals on sites like Groupon or LivingSocial, which raise visibility for price-related incentives in the mobile space.

5. To take in-store promotions one-step further and remind customers of advertised deals or create special incentives for mobile users, location based marketing will reach customers when they are in within range of a physical store location. This is achieved when messages are sent to the phone via Bluetooth or Infrared technologies but has limited range. Mobile coupons tied to location technology deliver redemption rates that are far superior to any other delivery mechanism.

6. If you have access to your customers' mobile telephone numbers, you can send them a text message to promote an offer. If you have promoted to the mobile list previously, you can create an intriguing follow-up message with an attractive new offer.

7. If you do not have a telephone list of your customers, how about using your other marketing channels, such as Twitter or Facebook? You can use these other channels to encourage your customers to interact with your brand by sending a text message to a short code number to get a special offer.

8. When users send the text message a computer replies with a code or password they can give the cashier to receive the discount. This is a good way to build up a list of mobile phone numbers that you can use later with other more targeted text messaging campaigns.

9. Make sure people are able to opt-in to your marketing messages by sending the recipients a text message that also confirms their number and makes the offer, like this: "Our customer database lists this mobile phone number. Reply with 'OK' to receive coupons & other messages at this number". You should also enable people to opt-out of receiving messages by sending the word "STOP" back to you.

Applications (apps)

There are hundreds of thousands of applications flooding the market, none of which work on every kind of device, but all of which must vie for a customer's limited attention. App marketing allows marketers to not only advertise around apps created by other people, but even to create their own apps which embed their brand deep within their customers' lives. Should you choose to create your own app, strive for content that is useful and brilliantly executed, as well as, of course, being useful. Think about how you can enhance the daily activities and/or situations of your target customers, whether it's looking after their children or running to lose weight. One company has a stand-alone app that does not sell anything but is actually very useful for customers. The North Face, which makes and sells outdoor sports clothing and gear, created a mobile phone app for skiers, which collects and displays local snow forecasts. The app is highly targeted because skiers are likely to purchase outdoor clothing, but it also serves as a geographically relevant need to understand local weather conditions – all from the convenience of a mobile phone. Every time a user checks the weather conditions for skiing, he will be reminded of The North Face brand. An important conclusion to draw from this is that, ultimately, this utility must come in the form of providing timely information or content that somehow relates to your brand positioning, promise or essence. You will also have a job in promoting your app if you go down this route, through internet marketing channels, word of mouth, advertising, finding a way to get your app listed in a 'Top apps' list, and PPC advertising. In fact, most of your money will be spent promoting your advertisment. This will invariably be a costly option. An alternative route to promoting your app is through Smore (**www.smore.com**). A service that helps small businesses build single page websites called 'flyers' – have recently announced their roll out of a new service that gives the same ability to app developers who are keen to build a single page mobile site to promote their apps. The service is aimed at small businesses and start-ups that do not have large advertising budgets to promote their apps. Smore for apps, though not 'fully launched' (still 'in beta') is available to try, as you will see from the screenshot below.

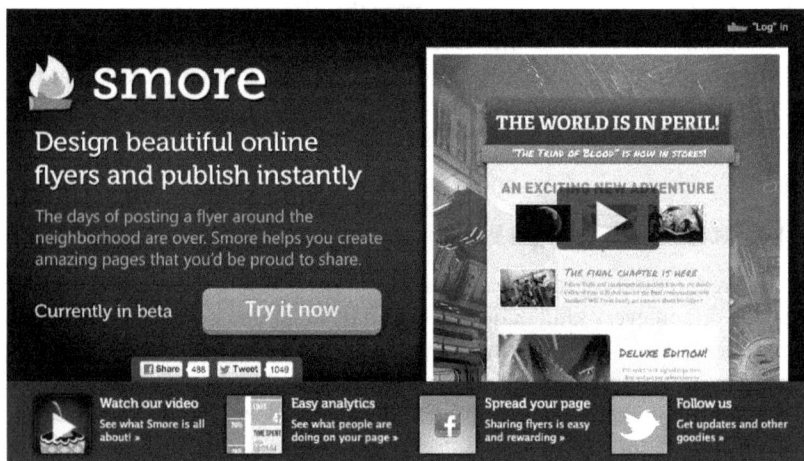

As well as offering the ability to quickly and easily build these sites, Smore offers promotional tools, including SEO optimisation and email compatibility. Users will also have the option of either using their own custom domain name or choosing a unique Smore address.

How to be successful in mobile marketing

Invest in a creative campaign – one that leverages multimedia. Incorporate a range of media, such as video and picture messages, in your campaign. Mobile games are also increasingly used by marketers. These games are now very sophisticated and popular with marketers taking advantage of this trend in several ways: in game ads, or fully branded sponsorship. Clearly though, the higher the impact – thanks to the use of multimedia – the more expensive the campaign, so consider your budget carefully. It's great to have a mobile campaign on the cheap and cheerful, but not if it fails to deliver and ends up being a waste of money. Invest in great execution – especially if a significant proportion of your visitors access your site via their mobile phones – so that you develop an engaging campaign for your users, regardless of which device they use. There are plenty of great mobile marketing agents out there to help with this, such as the well-respected Heart New Media (**www.heartnewmedia.com/mobile**). Google can also be a good first step in finding them, but make sure you also check out reviews of the marketing companies who you wish to use. A good company will make sure you follow best practice principles of mobile design; appreciate technical differences between devices, discuss with you the best layout, calls to action buttons and, most importantly, work with you to make sure you have no unnecessary content. When you are working with a mobile marketing company, make sure you discuss with them the following:

- **Make it easy for people to respond**. Give them something for their time, such as a voucher offering a discount.

- **Ensure your campaign is opt-in only**. This will be the best way to increase the chances of your success, as it will ensure that those who want your content are those who receive it.

- **Focus on usefulness**. Successful apps are those that are useful.

- **Use leverage technology**. With more and more mobile phones incorporating GPS technology, think about how you can use location in your campaigns to give your targets the right messages, at the right time and place.

- **Keep your subject lines concise**. When viewing on a mobile device, it is the "From" line of your content that gets the most attention. Make sure the "From" line is a simple representation of your company – and that your recipient will recognise it. Do not repeat what is in the "From" line again in the subject line; it is a waste of subject line characters. Most email programmes display only the first 30 to 50 characters and most mobile devices only show the first 20 to 30 characters, so you have a limited amount of text to get your point across.

Tips

- On mobile devices, the most effective subject lines are those where the immediate benefit often includes demonstrating that the email is useful on a mobile device. Use specifics to entice and motivate your audience to take your desired action. Here are some examples of motivating subject lines:
    - 30% coupon in this email (retailer).
    - Free entry coupon with this email (retailer).
    - All UK destinations on sale (travel company).
    - 24-hour sale starts today (retailer).

Quick summary

- Mobile is here to stay.
- At its most basic, mobile is SMS-based. However, there is a spectrum of complexity, from apps to location-based marketing.
- The main benefits of mobile marketing are in its reach, responsiveness, user engagement, data collection and portability. Mobile campaigns are also generally quick and easy for consumers to enter when out and about.

Conclusion

Internet marketing offers as many opportunities as it does challenges. The internet-enabled technological revolution has many implications for marketers. First, the digital consumer is more difficult to pin down. They are the 'new empowered', who will, through their privacy settings, block outs, opt-ins/opt-outs and on-demand technologies, see only the messages which they believe are relevant to them. Yet these consumers are indeed spending more time engaged with the web. No longer satisfied with just checking email, digital consumers are searching on various search engines for content; they are spending ever increasing amounts of time on social networking platforms such as YouTube and Facebook, and other equally immersive digital platforms, including their smartphones.

In this book, I have walked you through the most important elements of your online marketing plan, which is powered by three vital themes: having excellent content, making sure your content gets found through either organic search or paid search, and measuring the impact of your efforts through Google Analytics (or similar) for the continuous improvement of your performance. So, there is a little more to success than simply showing up on Google. Although, that is a big step in the right direction.

Good luck, I wish you all the best.

Useful Resources

Blogging resources

One of the significant benefits of using WordPress is that there are many plug-ins which are available to help you optimise your WordPress blog. Some of these plug-ins will help you to improve your visitors' experiences when reading your blog, whilst others will customise the performance of your blog. Visit Wordpress (**www.wordpress.org**) and search for the plug-ins to locate these:

Akismet – This must-have plug-in helps you to reduce your spam comments. It will stop what it detects to be spam and then holds these comments in a special moderation queue, separate from your other comments. You will be asked to review these comments and either delete or keep them.

Share This – Another useful plug-in which allows readers to add your blog posts to social bookmarking sites, through an icon that appears at the end of each of your posts. Readers can then click on the icon to select the social bookmarking site they want to share it on.

Yet Another Related Posts Plug-in – This is a great plug-in which has the potential to reduce your bounce rate (when a visitor leaves your site immediately, without viewing any other pages). The plug-in lists related posts to the one you have just written at the end of your post.

WordPress Database Backup – Avoid the tragedy of losing your hard work by getting this plug-in which backs up the core information in your blog. There is also the WordPress Database (WP-DB) Manager plug-in that lets you further customise your backups.

Subscribe to Comments – This is a popular plug-in that leverages the power of blog commenting. It allows readers to check a box when they leave a comment on your blog to subscribe to future comments. If they do this, they will receive emails notifying them when other comments are left on the post, so that they can continue with the conversation.

GoogleXML Sitemaps Generator – This essential plug-in lets you create a sitemap in no time at all. A sitemap has two key benefits; as your site expands it will enable readers to find posts, and it also helps the big search engines such as Google and Yahoo! to find, crawl and index your blog changes quickly.

Contact Form 7 – This is a neat way of allowing visitors to contact you. The plug-in uses two spam filters, Akismet and CAPTCHA, to make sure you only receive legitimate emails from humans!

Plug-ins to help you boost your blog traffic

All in One SEO Pack – This great plug-in allows you to add title tags (meaning you can be more interesting with the titles that your visitors see on your blog posts), descriptions, keywords, and more to every page and post published on your blog which is picked up by the search engines.

TweetThis – Another useful plug-in that increases the chances of visitors to your blog sharing your posts through Twitter, and so potentially increasing blog traffic. When you install the plug-in, an invitation link is included at the end of your blog posts inviting readers to "Tweet this" and share a link to the post they are reading through their Twitter feed.

WP-E-mail – Another 'sociable' plug-in. When you install it, a message and link are included at the end of every post, enabling visitors to email posts they like to others.

Making money from your blog – plug-ins to help you do this

There are a range of available plug-ins to be found on WordPress (**www.wordpress.org**) which are designed to help you increase the earning potential of your blog. Try these:

WP125 – This plug-in enables you to easily publish 125px by 125px (called the 'square button' size) ads on your blog. Upload, change, deactivate and maintain them very easily. It works well with the Thesis WordPress theme. For a complete list of WordPress ecommerce plug-ins visit **bit.ly/eTEkwZ**.

AdSense Manager – This plug-in helps you to place and maintain Google AdSense ads on your blog. The plug-in automatically generates AdSense code for your blog and allows you to use widgets to place and move ads around your blog.

Smart Ads – This automatically inserts advertisements, like Google's AdSense, above and below your post content. These advertisements are only visible when viewing a single post. As it doesn't make sense to fill small posts with adverts, users can set a "word count" minimum for their advertisements. Smart Ads will only insert advertisements into posts that meet or exceed the desired word count. You can also choose to only place advertisments on posts that are over a certain amount of days old. Advertisements can be manually disabled on a post-by-post basis, while writing a post, by category, or for registered blog members.

Shopping cart resources

Reduce friction for your customers by making it very easy for them to buy from you. Try the following shopping cart providers:

- CubeCart (**www.cubecart.com**)
- Zen Cart (**www.zen-cart.com**)
- Frooition (**www.frooition.com**)

Self-publishing resources

Self-publish your content on sites. Offer free and downloadable versions to potential customers.

- Lulu (**www.lulu.com**)
- Blurb (**www.blurb.com**)
- Snapfish by HP (**www.snapfish.co.uk**)

Resources to interact with others

You can also demonstrate a process by using a webinar or visual presentation where a live audience can see you and interact.

- GoToMeeting (**www.gotomeeting.com**)
- GoToWebinar (**www.gotowebinar.com**)
- Dimdim (**www.dimdim.com**)

Resources to produce a film

Showcase your products or expertise. Upload the film onto video sharing sites:

- YouTube (**www.youtube.com**)
- Vimeo (**www.vimeo.com**)

Resources to produce a podcast

There will be some customers who prefer to listen to your proposition or content. Upload a podcast packed with useful information, such as top tips, interviews or industry news. Podcasts can be recorded for free using the following sites:

- Skype (**www.skype.com**)
- Pamela Call Recorder (**www.pamela.biz**)

Your podcast can be edited using:

- Audacity (**www.audacity.sourceforge.net**)

Upload your podcast onto your website, as well as the following sites, to make sure you receive the widest possible audience:

- iTunes (**www.apple.com/itunes/podcasts/specs.html**)
- Podcast Alley (**www.podcastalley.com**)
- AudioBoo (**www.audioboo.com**)

Resources to develop an app

Make an app with your great content using the browser-based platform Appmakr. It is free to use and you can either set a list price to make money from it via the App store or make it available free of charge:

- Appmakr (**www.appmakr.com**)

Resources to form groups

Gather with like-minded people by forming groups:

- Facebook (**www.facebook.com**)
- LinkedIn (**www.linkedin.com**)
- Ning (**www.ning.com**)

Guest blog

Blog for other people and develop a following for your content:

- MyBlogGuest (**www.myblogguest.com**)

Resources to enable social sharing of your content

Have your content Stumbled, Digged or Tweeted to encourage the viral nature of social media. Add social sharing buttons to your site, to make it easier for visitors to share your content. Social bookmarking sites include:

- Delicious (**www.delicious.com**)
- Digg (**www.digg.com**)
- StumbleUpon (**www.stumbleupon.com**)
- Twitter (**www.twitter.com**)
- Flickr (photo sharing) (**www.flickr.com**)
- Lockerz Share (**www.addtoany.com**)

Resources for images

Below are lists of sites that will allow you to download and use images on your blogs. However, it is still important to read through the Terms of Use to ensure you are using them appropriately. Some of the free photos on these sites may require you to provide attribution, notify the photographer of your use of their photo or more. Obtain any necessary permission!

- **Flickr (www.Flickr.com/creativecommons)**: A firm favourite, Flickr is a great site to find photos in all manner of categories for your blog, under their creative commons license. It is important to provide attribution and link back to the source of the photo.

- **Stock Xchange (www.sxc.hu)**: Another useful site for finding free photos to use on your blog. Different photos have different restrictions, so be sure to check the copyright and attribution requirements before you use a photo.

- **MorgueFile** (**www.morguefile.com**): Again, you will find a large selection of free photos you can use on your blog. You may have to ask for permission and you will also need to link back from your blog post to the source (common courtesy!).

- **Dreamstime** (**www.dreamstime.com**): Dreamstime boasts a very large selection of royalty free photos, as well as images available for a fee.

- **Picapp** (**www.picapp.com**): A great idea with a clever premise; Picapp allows you free access to high resolution, quality images from the likes of Getty Images, Jupiter Images and more. All you do is search the Picapp database, copy the code provided and pastes it into your blog post HTML editor and publish it on your post. The image you selected will appear in your post with a gadget strip. When this gadget strip is clicked by a reader, they will be taken to another web page where related images and adverts appear. No such thing as a free lunch! Take a look at the Terms and Conditions before you use the images here. Image owners receive a royalty each time the image is used by a blogger and viewed by visitors.

Internet Marketing Jargon Buster

A

AB testing

AB testing, or split testing, refers to the practice of using two different versions of a page, or a page element, such as a heading, image or button. It is aimed at increasing page or site effectiveness metrics, such as click-through rates and conversions.

Above the fold

Above the fold refers to the most important content or advertising that is displayed on a web page without the need for a customer or visitor to scroll.

Ad impression

An ad impression refers to each time a consumer is exposed to an advertisement.

Ad rotation

This refers to the rotating of advertisements on a website for different user sessions.

Affiliate marketing

An affiliate is either a website owner or publisher who displays an advertisement (such as a banner or link) on his site for a merchant (the brand or the advertiser). When a purchaser visiting the affiliate's site clicks on this advertisement and goes onto perform a specified action (usually a purchase) on an advertiser's site, then the affiliate receives a commission.

Algorithm

The rules by which search engines decide on the relevance of a web page (and therefore ranking) in their organic search results.

Anchor text (for SEO)

A clickable link with text, which is important to search engine optimisation because it suggests to search engines the nature of the content of the page it refers to.

Attrition rate

The percentage of site visitors that is lost at each stage in making a purchase.

B

Bandwidth

The transmission rate of a communication line – usually measured in kilobytes per second (Kbps). The amount of data that can be carried per second by an internet connection.

Banner

A horizontal, online advert, usually found running across the top of a page in a fixed placement.

Blog

An online space, regularly updated, presenting the opinions or activities of oneself or a group of individuals.

Brand advocate

A customer who has favourable perceptions of a brand and who will talk favourably about a brand to their acquaintances, to help generate awareness of the brand or to influence purchase intent.

C

Cache memory

The cache memory is used to store web pages users have seen already. When users re-visit those pages, they load more quickly because they come from the cache and don't need to be downloaded over the internet again.

Cached date

This is the date when the search robot last visited a page.

Cached pages

Google robots take a snapshot of each page visited as they crawl the web. These are stored and used as a backup if the original page is unavailable.

Call to action (CTA)

An invitation to carry out an action, following an explanation or piece of promotional material.

Classified advertising

Classified advertising is called such because it is generally grouped under headings classifying the product or service being offered (headings such as Accounting, Business, etc.) and is grouped entirely in a distinct section, which makes it distinct from display advertising.

Click to call

A service that enables a mobile user to initiate a voice call to a specified phone number by clicking on a link on a mobile internet site.

Click to play

These video adverts have an initial static image file, which is displayed to encourage users to click to view the full video. The play rate is the proportion of viewers who click.

Click-through

When a user interacts with an advertisement and clicks through to the advertiser's website.

Click-through rate (CTR)

This refers to the frequency of click-through as a percentage of impressions served. A common measure of advertising effectiveness.

Commission

An amount of income received by a publisher for some quantifiable action, such as selling an advertiser's product and/or service on the publisher's website.

Content management systems (CMS)

CMS are typically browser-based web applications running on a server. All enable users to readily add new pages within an existing page template, e.g. WordPress.

Contextual advertising

Advertising that is targeted to the content on the webpage being viewed by a user at that specific time.

Conversion rate
A highly important measure of success which in internet marketing refers to the proportion of visitors who perform a business' desired action as a result of direct or subtle requests either from marketers, advertisers or content creators. Conversion rate = number of desired actions performed ÷ total visits to the site.

Cookie
A small text file on the user's PC that identifies the user's browser, so that they are 'recognised' when they re-visit a site.

Cookie expiry period
The time stated in an affiliate marketing programme between when a visitor clicks the affiliate link and the sale is credited to the affiliate. Typically, these are 7, 30 or 90 days.

Cost per acquisition (CPA)
Cost to acquire a new customer.

Cost per click (CPC)
The amount paid by an advertiser for a click on their sponsored search listing.

Cost per mille (CPM) / Cost per Thousand (CPT)
This refers to the amount it costs to show the advert to one thousand viewers (CPM).

Customer profiling
This is the practice of using a website to find out a customer's specific interests and characteristics.

D

Deep-linking advert
This refers to linking beyond a home page to a page inside a website with content pertinent to the advert.

Domain name
The unique name of an internet site, e.g. **www.ihubbusiness.co.uk**.

Dynamic ad delivery
Based upon predetermined criteria, dynamic ad delivery is the process by which a mobile advertisement is delivered, via a campaign management platform, to a publisher's mobile content.

E

Ecommerce (Electronic Commerce)
Typically, this refers to business that takes place over electronic platforms, such as the internet.

F

Firewall software
Firewalls provide additional security for a computer or local network by preventing unauthorised access. They sit as a barrier between the web and your computer, in order to prevent hacking, viruses or unapproved data transfer.

Flash
A web design software that creates animation and interactive elements, which are quick to download.

Forum
A forum is any online community where visitors may read and post topics of common interest.

Frames
A frame is a structure that allows for the dividing of a webpage into two or more independent parts.

G

Geo-targeting
Geo-targeting is the process of only showing adverts to people on a website and in search engines, based on their physical location. This could be done using advanced technology that knows where a computer is located or by using the content of a website to determine what a person is looking for, e.g. someone searching for gym in West London.

Global Standard for Mobiles (GSM)
The set of standards covering one particular type of mobile phone system.

H

Hit
A hit is a single request from a web browser for a single item from a web server.

HTML
Hyper Text Markup Language is the set of commands used by web browsers to interpret and display page content to users.

I

Image ad
An image on a mobile internet site with an active link that can be clicked on by the subscriber. Once clicked, the user is redirected to a new page; another mobile internet site or other destination where an offer, or something similar, awaits them.

Inbound links
The links coming into a site from another site. Inbound links are an important factor in the ranking algorithms of search engines.

Internet service provider (ISP)
A company which provides users with the means to connect to the internet.

IP address
The numerical internet address assigned to each computer on a network, so that it can be distinguished from other computers. Expressed as four groups of numbers separated by dots.

IPA
Institute of Practitioners in Advertising (IPA) is the trade body representing advertising agencies in the UK.

K

Keywords
The words which searchers will use to search for the information they need online.

L

LAN (Local area network)
A group of computers connected together which are at one physical location.

Landing page (squeeze page)
The 'sales promotion' page or view to which a user is directed when they click on an active link embedded in a banner, web page, email or other view. A click-through lands the user on a landing page.

Lead
When an action is taken by a visitor, e.g. if they register, sign up for, or download something on your site, that action can be referred to as a lead.

Location based services (LBS)
Services that are offered to mobile subscribers, dependent on the geographical location of their handsets within their mobile network. LBS includes driving directions and information about certain resources within the current location, such as restaurants, ATMs, shopping, and so on.

Log files
A record of all the hits a web server has had over a given period of time.

M

Meta search engine
This is a search engine that displays results from multiple search engines.

Meta-tags/descriptions
HTML tags that identify the content of a web page for search engines.

Mobile internet advertising
Advertising via mobile phones or other wireless devices (excluding laptops). This type of mobile advertising includes mobile web banner adverts, mobile internet sponsorship, as well as mobile paid-for search listings. Mobile internet advertising does not include other forms of mobile marketing, such as SMS, MMS and short code.

MP3
A computer file format that compresses audio files up to a factor of 12 from a .wav file (an IBM and Microsoft audio file format standard for storing audio data streams on PCs).

MPEG
A file format used to compress and transmit video clips online.

N

Natural search results
These are also referred to as 'organic" search results and they appear in the search engine results listings in a separate section (usually the main body of the page) to the paid listings. They are referred to as organic or natural because they have not been paid for, and are ranked by the search engines using algorithms according to relevancy and other factors known to search engines.

O

Online video advertising
Video advertising that accompanies video content distributed via the internet, to be streamed or downloaded onto compatible devices, such as computers and mobile phones. In its basic form, this can be TV advertisments run online, but adverts are increasingly adapted or created specifically to suit online watchers. Video advertising can be placed before (pre-roll), during (mid-roll) and after (post-roll) video content.

Opt-in
An individual has given their agreement for their data to be used for marketing purposes.

Opt-out
An individual has stated that they do not want their data to be used for marketing purposes.

Outbound link
A link to an external site, i.e. outside of the current site.

Overlay
This is online advertising content that appears over the top of the webpage.

P

Paid for listings
The search results list in which advertisers pay to be featured according to the PPC model. This list usually appears in the search results listings in a separate section usually at the very top of the organic listings and at the top right hand side of the page:

Paid inclusion
In exchange for a payment, a search engine will guarantee to list/review pages from a website. It is not necessarily the case that the pages will rank well for particular queries – this still depends on the search engine's underlying relevancy process.

Pay for performance programme
Also called affiliate marketing, performance-based partner marketing, cost per action (CPA), or associate programme. It includes any type of revenue sharing programme where a publisher receives a commission for generating online activity (e.g. leads or sales), on behalf of an advertiser.

Pay per click (PPC)
Allows advertisers to bid for placement in the paid listings search results on terms that are relevant to their business. Advertisers pay the amount of their bid only when a consumer clicks on their listing. Also called sponsored search or paid search.

Pay per lead
The commission structure where the advertiser pays the publisher a flat fee for each qualified lead (customer) that is referred to the advertiser's website.

Pay per sale
The commission structure where the advertiser pays a percentage or flat fee to the publisher, based on the revenue generated by the sale of a product or service to a visitor who came from a publisher site.

Payment threshold
This refers to the minimum accumulated commission an affiliate must earn to trigger payment from an affiliate programme.

Podcasting
Podcasting involves making an audio file (usually in MP3 format) of content that is available to download.

Pop-under
An advertisment that appears in a separate window beneath an open window. Pop-under adverts are concealed until the top window is closed, moved, resized or minimised.

Pop-up
An online advert that 'pops up' in a window over the top of a web page.

R

Reach
The number of unique web users potentially seeing a website one or more times in a given time period, which is expressed as a percentage of the total active web population for that period.

Really simple syndication (RSS)
Software that allows users to flag website content (often from blogs or news sites) and aggregate new entries to this content into an easy-to-read format that is delivered directly to a user's computer.

Reciprocal links
An agreement to exchange links between two sites – thought to have little effect on search engine rankings.

Rich media
The collective name for online advertising formats that use advanced technology to harness broadband to build brands. Rich media uses interactive and audio-visual elements to give richer content and a richer experience for the user when interacting with the advert.

Run of network (RON)
An advertising option whereby advert placements can appear on any pages on sites within an ad network.

Run of site (ROS)
An advertising option whereby advert placements can appear on any pages of the target site.

S

Search engine marketing (SEM)
The process which aims to get websites listed prominently in search engine results, through search engine optimisation, sponsored search and paid inclusion.

Search engine optimisation (SEO)
The process which aims to get websites listed prominently within search engine's organic (algorithmic, spidered) search results. Involves making a site 'search engine friendly'.

Server
A host computer that maintains websites, newsgroups and email services.

Session
The time spent between a user starting an application, computer or website and logging off or quitting.

Site analytics
The reporting and analysis of website activity – in particular, user behaviour on the site. All websites have a weblog which can be used for this purpose, but other third party software is available for a more sophisticated service.

Skyscraper
A long, vertical, online advert, usually found running down the side of a page in a fixed placement.

Solus email advertising
Where the body of the email is determined by the advertiser, including both text and graphical elements, and is sent on their behalf by an email list manager/owner. Solus email advertising is conducted on an opt-in basis, where the recipient has given their consent to receive communications.

Spam
Unsolicited junk mail.

Spider
A programme which crawls the web and fetches web pages, in order for them to be indexed against keywords. Used by search engines to formulate search result pages.

Stickiness
This refers to the effectiveness of a site in retaining its users. Usually measured by the duration of the visit or the number of page views.

Streaming media
Compressed audio/video, which plays and downloads at the same time.

T

Text ad
A static appended text attached to an advertisement.

Traffic
Number of visitors who come to a website.

U

Uniform resource locator (URL)
Technical term that is used to refer to the web address of a particular website, e.g. **www.ihubbusiness.co.uk**.

Unique users
Number of different individuals who visit a site within a specific time period.

User generated content (UGC)
Online content created by website users rather than media owners or publishers – either through reviews, blogging, podcasting or posting comments, pictures or video clips. Sites that encourage user generated content include YouTube, Wikipedia and Flickr.

V

Video on demand (VOD)
Allows users to watch what they want, when they want. This can be either pay per view or a free service, usually funded by advertising.

Viral marketing
Refers to the idea that people will pass on and share exciting or outstanding content. Typically viral marketing is sponsored by a brand, which is looking to

build awareness of a product or service. Viral commercials often take the form of funny video clips, or interactive Flash games and images.

Voice over internet protocol (VOIP)
Technology that allows the use of a broadband Internet connection to make telephone calls.

W

WAP (Wireless Application Protocol)
WAP is the standard for providing mobile data services on hand-held devices. It delivers internet content, such as news, weather and travel information, to mobile phones and it can also be used to deliver formatted content such as wallpapers, ringtones, video, games, portals and other useful links.

Web 2.0
Web 2.0 identifies the consumer as a major contributor in the evolution of the internet into a two-way interactive medium.

Web based
Requiring no software to access an online service or function, other than a web browser and access to the internet.

Web portal
A website or service that offers a broad array of resources and services, such as email, forums, search engines, and online shopping malls.

Whitelist
An email whitelist is a list of contacts that the user deems are acceptable to receive email from and should not be sent to the trash folder.

Wi-Fi (wireless fidelity)
The ability to connect to the internet wirelessly. Internet 'hotspots' in coffee shops and airports, etc, use this technology.

Wiki
A type of website that allows visitors themselves to easily add, remove, and otherwise edit and change some available content.

X

XHTML (Extensible Hypertag Markup Language)
The language used to create most mobile internet sites.

XML (Extensible Markup Language)
Language used by many internet applications for exchanging information.

About Brightword Publishing

Brightword publishing is the small business imprint from Harriman House and Enterprise Nation. Brightword produces print books, kits and digital products aimed at a small business and start-up audience, providing high quality information from high profile experts in an accessible and approachable way.

Other Products from Brightword

49 Quick Ways to Market your Business for Free

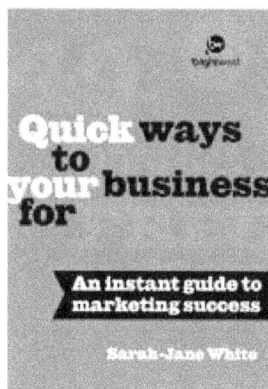

By Sarah-Jane White
eBook ISBN: 978-0-85719-144-1

50 Fantastic Franchises!

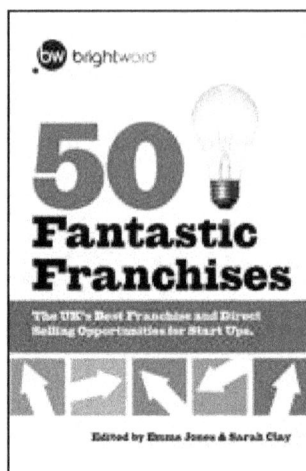

By Emma Jones and Sarah Clay
eBook ISBN: 978-1-90800-302-7

50 Top Tech Tools and Tips

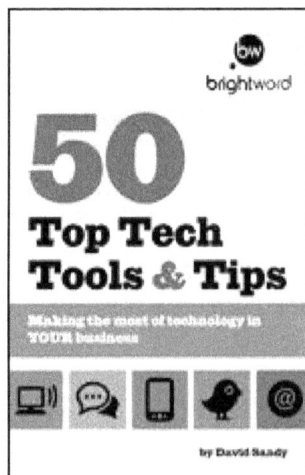

By David Sandy
eBook ISBN: 978-1-90800-324-9

Go Global: How to Take Your Business to the World

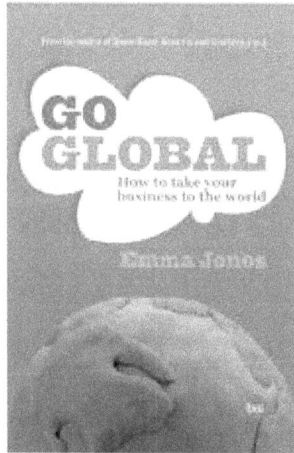

By Emma Jones
eBook ISBN: 978-1-90800-303-4
Print ISBN: 978-1-90800-300-3

Micro Multinationals

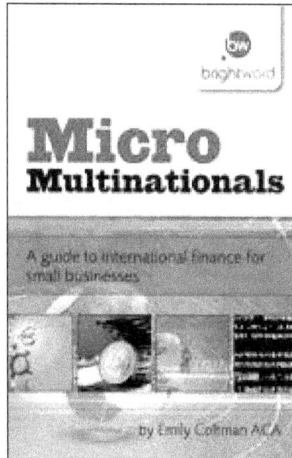

By Emily Coltman
eBook ISBN: 978-1-90800-328-7

Motivating Business Mums

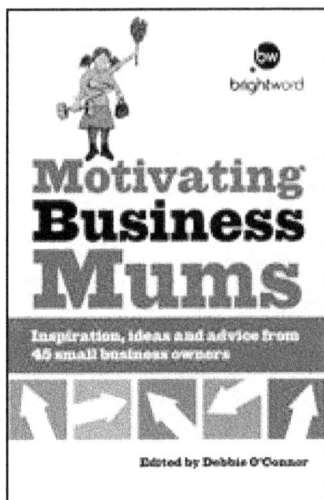

By Debbie O'Connor
eBook ISBN: 978-1-90800-309-6

The Start-Up Kit 2013: Everything you need to start a small business

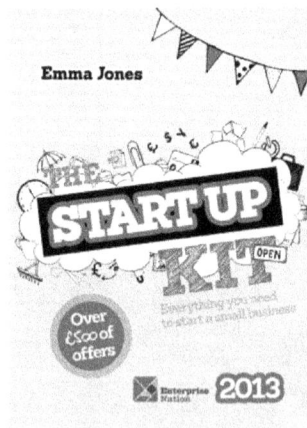

By Emma Jones
eBook ISBN: 978-1-90800-359-1

Turn Your Talent into a Business

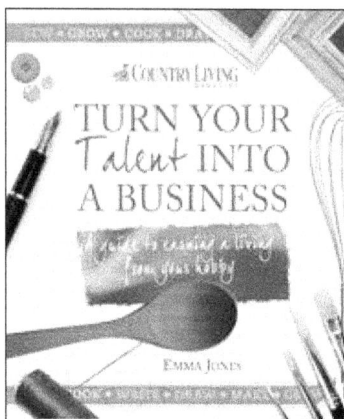

By Emma Jones
eBook ISBN: 978-1-90800-326-3
Print ISBN: 978-1-90800-323-2

Our Business Bites series

Contracts for Your Business

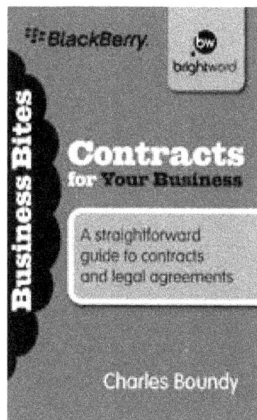

By Charles Boundy
eBook ISBN: 978-1-908003-16-
Print ISBN: 978-1-908003-21-8

Facebook for Business

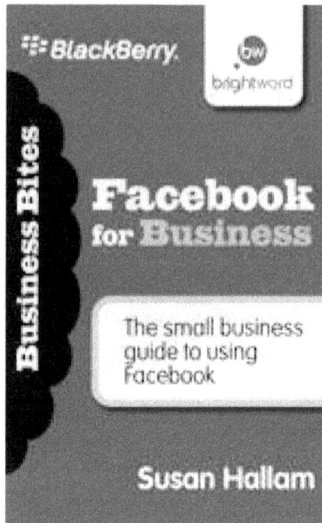

By Susan Hallam
eBook ISBN: 978-1-908003-13-3

Pitching Products For Small Business

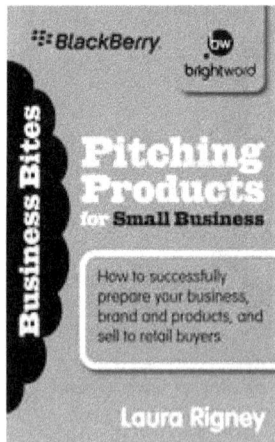

By Laura Rigney
eBook ISBN: 978-0-857190-41-3
Print ISBN: 978-1-908003-17-1

Twitter Your Business

By Mark Shaw
eBook ISBN: 978-1-90800-304-1

Selling for Small Business

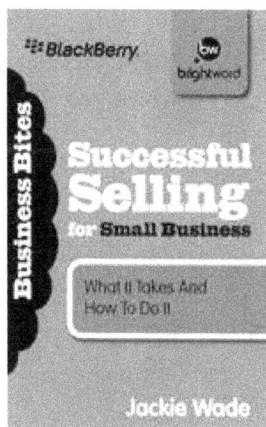

By Jackie Wade
eBook ISBN: 978-1-90800-308-9
Print ISBN: 978-1-908003-19-5

Finance for Small Business

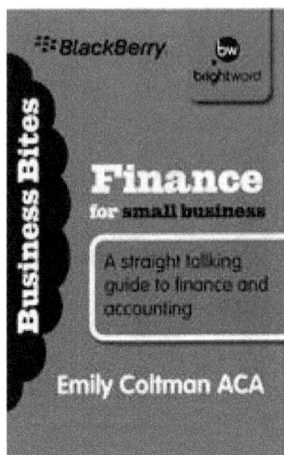

By Emily Coltman
eBook ISBN: 978-1-90800-306-5
Print ISBN: 978-1-908003-20-1

The Small Business Guide to Apps

By David Howell
eBook ISBN: 978-1-908003-10-2

The Small Business Guide to China

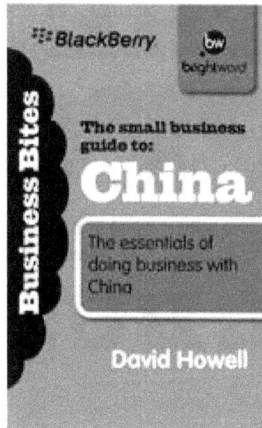

By David Howell
eBook ISBN: 978-1-908003-11-9
Print ISBN: 978-1-908003-22-5

The Small Business Guide to PR

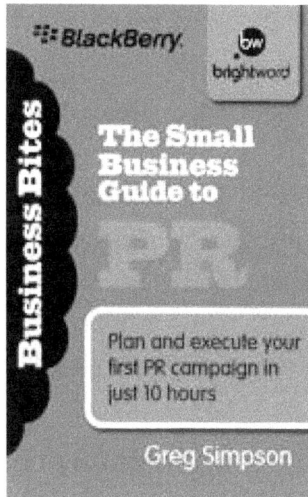

By Greg Simpson
eBook ISBN: 978-1-908003-33-1

GET THE BEST SUPPORT
FOR YOUR
SMALL BUSINESS

JOIN ENTERPRISE NATION: **A thoroughly modern business club**

- Free business eBooks
- Discounts on business events
- Exclusive business benefits – including access to over 1,000 workspaces in 85 countries

Enterprise Nation helps thousands of people turn their good ideas into great businesses.

We also represent your views in the heart of government.

So, take your business to the next level – with comprehensive support, including marketing help, networking opportunities and over £500-worth of exclusive business benefits.

Join the club now for just £20 per year – and get a FREE Enterprise Nation mug!

Find out more at **www.enterprisenation.com**